ODA

ODA
OFFICE of DESIGN and ARCHIT-ECTURE

Rizzoli
NEW YORK

New York · Paris · London · Milan

INTRODUCTION BY PAUL GOLDBERGER

The idea of apartment living is more deeply embedded in the identity of New York than any other city, at least in the United States, and yet no city has done as poorly as New York at creating an appealing architectural language out of which new apartment houses can be designed. There once was such a language, back in the years before World War II, and it tied the grandest apartments on Park Avenue, Fifth Avenue, and Central Park West together with middle class buildings in places like West End Avenue and the side streets of the Upper East Side and so much of Brooklyn and the Bronx. The buildings built then all respected the street; they had a gentle mix of Georgian or Gothic or Italian Renaissance detailing or perhaps even a hint of Art Moderne; and they had excellent floor plans that were crafted as skillfully as a Rubik's cube. They were easy on the eye and gracious to live in.

Until the 1950s, almost every building was designed to speak in one of the dialects of this architectural language. Then came the mean, cramped buildings of white brick, which in turn were followed by glass boxes, some of which were elegant to look at but worked much better as stand-alone objects than as parts of a larger, coherent urban whole. A few architects have tried to solve the problem by creating designs that replicate the look of buildings of the past, and while many of these, too, are elegant, even the best of them seems to carry the implicit message that our time has neither the ability nor the inclination to establish a common language for apartment design—a vernacular, as it were.

Into this confused mix comes ODA—Office of Design and Architecture—a firm that seems not to have given up on the idea that a building can be new and very much a part of the twenty-first century, and yet at the same time be designed as a part of the larger streetscape and cityscape, not as a one-off object. ODA and its founding partner, Eran Chen, have taken it upon themselves to try to establish a new version of the architectural language that we have been missing. Their buildings do not look like the apartment houses of the 1920s, and neither are they glass boxes. They are generally not boxes at all, or at least not big, simple boxes. It is probably more accurate to describe most of ODA's designs as assemblages of boxes, full of setbacks and cutouts and roof terraces; an ODA building almost invariably has a lively profile, and they tend to be more sculptural where it is important to be visually exciting, up in the sky, and somewhat plainer where it is more important to be direct and straightforward, at the street level. They are complex, lively compositions, and by now there are enough of them so that they have begun to constitute their own vernacular, the language we have been looking for: respectful of the street and the skyline both, a balance of masonry and glass, made up of straight lines and right angles more than curves or diagonals. The effect is neither flamboyant nor quiet, but pleasantly in between.

You can see something of Moshe Safdie's Habitat 67 in Montreal in some of what Eran Chen designs in the way that many of ODA's buildings seem to be like stacked blocks, mounting from a large base to a lively assemblage of cubes toward the top. Habitat, of course, was envisioned as a prototype, as a partially prefabricated system that might be expanded to create an improved standard for multifamily housing. Its greatest success, however, was in its appearance, not its structural system, and ODA has picked up on that aesthetic, using it as the inspiration for market-rate housing in which the details are more lavish, and the materials more carefully considered, than in Habitat, now a piece of architectural history. But in ODA's work there are also welcome connections to the industrial aesthetic of both the late nineteenth and early twentieth centuries, as well as to the glass curtain wall buildings that still constitute the modernist orthodoxy.

When you look at an ODA building, you perceive a sculptural presence, and you perceive an urbanistic presence: maybe that is the key thing, the ability of this architecture to be simultaneously an object in itself and an object that seems shaped by, and responsive to, its urban context. Too often, these two sides of urban architecture—the sculptural and the contextual—are seen as a kind of zero-sum game, as if to say that the more compelling a building's shape is, the less it is likely to have anything to do with its surroundings.

ODA seems intent on proving this wrong, and it does. All its buildings have shapes that catch the eye, but the forms are never arbitrary or excessive. They are lively, but not to the point of showing indifference to their surroundings. Some of them, like 15 Renwick in Manhattan and 1040 Dean in Brooklyn, are extremely well-behaved, and defer to the street more than show off their shape; others, like Bevel in Long Island City, Queens, and 101 West 14th Street in Manhattan, are more striking, not to say assertive, as forms, but they never come off as excessive, as form for form's sake. The goal, it would seem, is to be bold enough to catch your eye, but not so forceful as to deny the building's role as part of a

larger urban whole. It is a kind of equilibrium that ODA strives for, and usually achieves.

You can see that in the way that this book has been organized, its chapters moving from Apartment to Building to Block to Neighborhood. The message, of course, is that nothing, not the individual apartment or the building or the block or even the neighborhood, exists in isolation. Each is a part of a larger whole, and everything within that whole relates in some way to everything else, or it should. Relating does not mean imitating, but it means being able to live comfortably together, and to recognize that the goal of architecture is not just the making of comfortable and visually pleasing places in which to live, but the making of community.

For all that Eran Chen and his colleagues want to make a coherent and readable architectural language and to have their buildings coexist comfortably with their surroundings, they should not be mistaken for timid. Their body of work contains buildings like 10 Jay Street in Dumbo, for example, an altogether remarkable renovation of a nineteenth-century brick industrial building facing the East River. ODA restored three sides of the building faithfully, and from the street it is hard to think that it is anything other than a well-kept historical relic. But the side facing the East River is entirely new, an explosion of reflective glass designed to evoke sugar crystals, a nod to the building's origins as the Arbuckle sugar refinery. Here, the equilibrium ODA sought is not between urbanism and sculpture; it is between past and present, and between the intimate urbanism of the streetscape, where the restored brick facades are viewed at close range, and the distant urbanism of the riverfront, where the new and frankly flamboyant glass facade is a strong signpost of the new when viewed from across the river.

And then there is the Torch, the hotel and entertainment tower proposed for midtown Manhattan that widens at the top to contain restaurants, has a narrow midsection that will contain a "free-fall" thrill ride, and a relatively conventional skyscraper base. It is an unusual form, to say the least, and to some it may appear that ODA's embrace of the new has gone too far. If nothing else, the building celebrates the cacophony of the theater district, where architecture has never been genteel. It is no accident that the pages of this book show it in the context of recent Manhattan skyscrapers, since its very wildness is a response to the explosive growth of the skyline over the last generation, and to the continuing determination of architects and developers to find new ways to break out of the restraints of the modernist box.

And ODA continues to do that, not just in Manhattan but in Washington, D.C., where the firm has completed several buildings that play major roles in establishing the Wharf area and the area around Nationals Park. And the same can be said for ODA's towers on the Williamsburg waterfront in Brooklyn, and in its plans for large-scale projects as far afield from its New York base as Moscow, Rotterdam, and Buenos Aires. Whether in Washington or Williamsburg, Brooklyn or Buenos Aires, in each instance ODA's work shows formal inventiveness, a willingness to solve problems, and most important of all, a recognition that no building is purely an object in itself, but a part of a larger urban whole.

FORM FOLLOWS FUN

BY ERAN CHEN

It's been well over a century since the phrase form follows function was coined by Louis Sullivan. Even though the functionalist approach to architecture is mostly associated with the Modernist Era (and has been hotly debated ever since), my take is that "function" has in fact been the focus of our profession and still is.

Fueled in America by the Second Industrial Revolution, our focus on functionality has been carried on by modern architects and urban planners for the past century as we try and accommodate the needs of people moving to our cities. While the growth of modern America has helped create a burgeoning middle class and a global economy, one might argue it has lessened the joy—or even the fun—of living. We are now at a place where cities are shrinking, our infrastructure is suffering, and we need to reinvent our urban cores as an enjoyable destination that can still meet our ever-changing needs.

Form Follows FUNction

Fun may seem like an odd metric for an architect. But especially in today's digital age, where many functions are handled virtually, fun deserves a closer look as a foundation for the work we do.

Today, the Internet provides most of our daily services—from retail and banking to healthcare—and increasingly supplements our social interactions. How can we reinforce or reinvent the physical realm? What is the role of walkable, mixed-use streetscapes as a way of building vibrant urban communities? Or are these merely romantic ideas about street culture, popularized by the New Urbanism of the late twentieth century? Have they run their course in an era when denizens of urban environments no longer need to go outside for provisions and social activities? While there is no question that times have changed, the big challenge now is how to make cities and street-level experiences that can offer a valuable counterpart to our virtual realm.

I, for one, am not ready to give up on the urban dream that drew me to architecture in the first place—the idea of street

culture as the glue that holds together an urban environment—or the professional mission of fostering our streets as the spine that supports the city culture and community that we're all a part of.

As architects, we've been in the habit of designing singular buildings that consider only the everyday experiences of its tenants—whether these are single family townhouses, multiunit housing complexes, office towers, or hotels. But how do buildings come together to shape the urban experience? It's going to mean thinking outside the box, in a more holistic way than we're used to as siloed practitioners. We'll have to push the envelope. Or, as I like to say (at risk of further muddying these expressions), expand the envelope.

EXPANDING THE ENVELOPE

Architecture is tectonic; it's about creating form and shaping our future. As architects, we use walls, roofs, ceilings, and floors to envelop three-dimensional space and control light. And we do it, almost always, with an eye toward geometric efficiency.

That is why cities have predominantly used squares and rectangles to streamline and optimize their structures both horizontally and vertically. Efficiency also explains why most cities are organized the way they are, with the urban landscape broken up into rectangular plots. It's clean, easy to sell and trade, and cost-effective.

At ODA, we are certainly not anti-efficiency. That would be silly and self-defeating. Nor do we dismiss functionality as a top priority. But we are also committed to the quality of life that stems from our ability to connect, to experience, to enjoy and bringing people together. We cannot design *only* for geometric efficiency and rectilinear functionality. We need opportunities for exploration and discovery—unexpected moments that break through the grid.

Likewise, when it comes to the future of cities and how we want to build, I maintain that we can do better, tectonically, with designs that increase exposure to light, air, outdoor spaces, and to one another (more on that shortly).

It's not possible to rebuild our great cities from scratch. And for the most part, our vision for this kind of envelope expansion involves using existing infrastructure to maximize the public realm and bring more green spaces to our urban environment. We must focus on the exciting adaptions we can implement gradually to our existing structures.

How? Specifically, this can be achieved by granting new air rights to existing buildings in exchange for opening their courtyards to the public—the logic being that the commercial value of private space is dependent on lively, diverse, and accessible public areas. In other words, the active ground floor adds immeasurably to whatever is built above, creating both quality-of-life and economic incentives.

In this way, we reinvent the physical public realm in high-density cities, space by space, building by building, block by block, neighborhood by neighborhood, and ultimately we can bring about something of a revolution in the way we all experience our urban environments.

Over the following chapters, we look closely at how this envelope-expanding approach to architecture plays out on micro and macro levels, at four different "scales": (1) the individual unit, (2) the whole building (3) the city block that the building is on, and (4) the many blocks that form the neighborhood.

Each of the scales builds on what came before. By expanding the envelope in how we design an individual apartment—such as pushing and pulling areas within the space to increase exposure to light and carving outdoor spots—we create buildings (i.e., clusters of apartment units) that expand the envelope. Or, by taking four or five buildings and connecting them with a surrounding courtyard, we open up the heart of a whole city block. In aggregate, these blocks can transform entire neighborhoods.

Maybe at this point we should say that "expansion of the functional" is about generosity rather than waste, about connections to nature and one another. It's the true sustainability of our communities.

At the risk of sounding simplistic, if architecture is about creating form, there is an almost Russian-doll quality to the forms we create at different thresholds. Ultimately, the form of making an individual apartment is similar to the form of making a neighborhood. Through the various examples we use in this book you'll see exactly how this repeating, fractal-like dynamic works. First, we expand the envelope in our design of an individual unit, then we duplicate that idea at bigger and bigger scales.

But it's not just about shapes and forms. At the center of all these ideas is the most important element: people.

THE HUMAN ELEMENT

Our ultimate vision for expanding the urban envelope is about creating pockets of human interaction across different scales. Think about your own living situation—your apartment, your block, your neighborhood. Consider what is happening within these different spheres. First, of course, you have your personal life that you live inside your home, perhaps with your family or friends. Then there are the interactions with your neighbors in your building, and in your neighborhood. How would you characterize your experiences with these different groups?

As an architect, it gives me great satisfaction to think about these layers of social connection and how to give form to each. Especially in the context of our digital age, where in-person interaction has become largely a matter of choice rather than necessity, it gets my creative juices flowing to consider: what are the human experiences of everyday life that have been lost and how can we use our existing infrastructure to bring people together and create new experiences and pockets of overlap? Moreover, how can we inject some fun back into our shared activities and interactions? What can we use that is free? Air and light are free; connection and interaction; love and happiness; fun is free.

Our mission, then, is to construct, block by block, joyful streetscapes that draw people out to enjoy the richness of in-person experiences. And by repeating or replicating this endeavor—formally, aesthetically, and philosophically—at each scale, we see how a snowball effect can start to occur, an accumulation of excitement and human vitality at the street level.

Green spaces, free and open to all, are an important ingredient but they're not everything. In order for, say, a public courtyard to achieve its full potential, it needs to be supported by indoor attractions, including but not limited to traditional retail. Affordability is key. Think markets filled with diverse local vendors. But that's only the tip of the iceberg. More than just shopping, it's about people coming together for a true cultural experience. From sports-related activities to urban farming, from playgrounds to wellness centers, the idea is to transform our streetscapes into places that meet our functional needs and forge deeper paths of discovery.

With their menagerie of unique spaces for working, living, shopping, and eating, mixed-used structures and complexes can stand out in a big way from traditional efficiency-driven urban architecture. Varying scales and a sense of ambiguity is what makes it all work, a feature of this new model for the public realm—one that invites people to explore with no particular agenda.

In the end, what these streetscapes offer, with their multifunctional environments and creative programming, is something fresh and exciting that still feels familiar, intimate, inviting to all—and fun.

APART

A number of years ago, I was looking for an apartment to rent in Paris and was struck by the vivid language used in the listings. The descriptions on French real estate websites read almost like literature, filled with words such as "magical" and "romantic." The verbiage went beyond the basic specs and amenities to what it actually *felt* like to live in the apartment: "After you ascend the wooden staircase, you enter the sun-kissed living room…" In perusing these listings, I was transported into the physical spaces described. And one of my favorite things about the listings was how they always made sure to mention how far you are from the closest baguette shop!

On the one hand, the flats I was looking at in Paris were not so far removed from their Manhattan counterparts: space is a premium in both housing markets and apartments are often very small. But the focus in France is less on the square footage or functionality of the unit and much more on the *experience*, the sensation of, say, standing on your dormer looking over the zinc roofs of the neighboring buildings.

In New York, however, we've somehow grown accustomed to banality, thinking about apartment living in almost entirely pragmatic terms. We've been trained to accept that all that really matters is size and location. How did this happen? When did we become the mice of this city? And what can we learn from our Gallic friends and their focus on experience?

THE EXPERIENCE OF APARTMENT LIFE

First, we must ask ourselves, what *is* the experience of living in a city apartment? What are some of the ways this form and space can interact with our senses? For example, I love bay windows, especially on lower floors in a south-facing apartment in the afternoon, where I can get inside the window, look outside, and curl up in the sun's warmth. This "magical moment" is a concept I've found useful in thinking about the bigger goal of redefining quality of life in urban environments—and putting the *fun* into function.

We know that cities are expensive, high-density, and a challenge when it comes to quality of life (at least, as traditionally defined). Living in a city apartment, chances are you're going to have significantly less space than you would in a similarly priced house in the suburbs. These factors, and the sheer intensity of city life, mean that we must intentionally design and curate magical moments and pay greater care in composing those experiences. We need windows deep enough to sit within, those which create wider exposures and allow us to see more of the street life below. We should wisely use what is free and fun—light and air are free, visual connections are free.

What you typically hear when looking at apartments in big cities—what usually are considered the important criteria—is far more rudimentary. As architects, I want to go beyond this baseline commitment to efficiency and this limited understanding of the functions required for city living. If unintentionally we're the ones who created this sad state of affairs—where experience, fun, beauty, and connection have all but disappeared from our residential expectations within the city culture and community we're all a part of—then imagine what we can do with the right intention.

AN EMOTIONAL EXPERIENCE

We designed a rental building in Brooklyn's Bushwick neighborhood where we installed boxes outside the door of every single apartment. Some of the boxes were made from glass, others from wood, others from concrete. The idea was that people could decorate them as they wish, putting a part of who they are in the shared space of the corridor. Some tenants put flowers in them, others put seashells, one apartment used the box to promote their home business, others showcased pictures of their dogs.

When residents walk around, they get to see all the different boxes reflecting the distinct personalities of each of their neighbors, while making their own apartment feel less anonymous. Every time they come home, they're greeted at the threshold by this symbol that means something special to them.

The "threshold," a space that allows for transition from one point to another, is one of the most important elements in architecture; it is an *experience* all its own, driven by the anticipation or mental preparation leading up to it, as well as the contrast or tension between what lies on one side and the other. The threshold is one of the best tools we have for creating "magical moments."

A threshold could be a door, window, porch, vestibule, or really any space that constitutes a transformative moment between one condition and another. In the case of our ornamental boxes, we used that threshold to create a moment of distinction (from apartment door to corridor) as well as an emotional moment of discovery.

OUTDOOR SPACES

Outdoor spaces like balconies or terraces are similarly ripe with threshold potential.

An outdoor balcony or terrace is usually thought of only as a place to be out in the open. Rarely do we think of it as a threshold between inside and out, as a transitional, in-between place.

But a small balcony or terrace can be designed so it's set back or integrated and feels very much like part of the living space, while also part of the outside. There's a visual and mental expansion that happens where the outdoor area becomes almost like another room, an extension of your city apartment experience and quality of life.

It's not dissimilar to the role the porch plays in the architecture of the American south. A southern-style porch just means the deck in front of your house is covered on top and furnished with rocking chairs and such. When you're sitting out on a porch like this, you're not inside but neither are you out—yet you are both inside and out. No wonder the American porch became a symbol in films and literature as a place of deep deliberation, contemplation, and love. The same idea is seen in the brownstone neighborhoods of Brooklyn, where you have the threshold of the stoop, a place where people sit and talk to their neighbors, where they read their morning paper. When you're on your stoop, are you home? Or are you outside? The answer is you're somewhere in between, in the beautiful, uncommitted transitional space.

You can have the same experience even on a high-density Manhattan block with an apartment balcony. It's about exploring the possibilities for using this threshold to create a magical moment of transition where, for example, you feel like you're outside when the door is open, even though you're inside. If you can create a terrace with two doors, one from the living room and one from the bedroom, you'll get a kind of cross-view of the outdoor space, which contributes to that feeling of it being another room in your apartment rather than just a jumping board at the edge.

Within the dense urban grid of New York, we may not be able to get a baguette as easily as in Paris, but we *can* have a city-apartment experience that's about more than square footage, that touches our emotions and what makes us human.

We can still be pragmatic and efficient, while *also* creating moments of beauty and pleasure, no matter the size of apartment, around how we actually experience the space with our five senses. We can take this element of experience and make it part of our design. We can even make apartment living *fun*.

And in doing so, over time we can change our cultural set of expectations when it comes to quality of life in urban environments, so that people who live in small apartments in big cities can find their own kind of poetry in their living spaces.

LOCATION	10 Hubert Street, New York, NY
CLIENT	Undisclosed
SIZE	5,300 SF
TEAM	Eran Chen, P. Christian Bailey, Ryoko Okada, Kris Levine

10 HUBERT

A city like New York seems forever active with new development, the skyline ever changing. But the city is simultaneously rich with historic districts, like Tribeca and Soho, where landmark status preserves the original urban fabric, and where new renovation work can serve to celebrate the layered narratives of the city as it has evolved over the last centuries. As a conservation project, the goal behind the renovation of 10 Hubert Street was to return the space to its original design, channeling Tribeca's commercial atmosphere, while updating it into a light-filled residential loft with direct access to outdoor space.

The five-story Romanesque Revival brick building at 10 Hubert was originally designed in 1892 by Julius Kastner as store and warehouse for liquor importer J. H. Bearns & Co. It remained a commercial building well into the late twentieth century, housing a variety of tenants over the course of a hundred years, but by the early 1990s, much of the building's brick and terracotta ornamentation was damaged, the original cornice removed, and the cast iron storefront filled in.

The newly restored facades of Hubert and Collister Streets include the foliate moldings, cornices, and arched windows. We used a minimal color palette and maintained and upgraded the original characteristics. Inside, a steel catwalk with glass floors is attached to the walls of the double-height living area and allows for a wraparound library. On the roof of the building, a 1,000-square-foot penthouse was added, but carefully designed to be invisible to pedestrians and respectful of the historic community. This addition is clad with standing seam zinc and steel windows, wooden doors, and steel railings, offering an unintrusive new connection to exterior urban living.

The former store and warehouse building at 10 Hubert was renovated to celebrate the original late nineteenth-century architecture.

Located on the street side of the building, the living space is opened up as a double-height space, defined by a steel and glass gallery mezzanine.

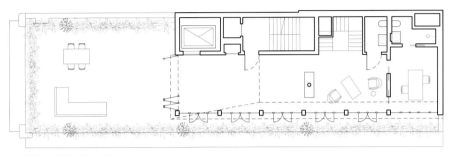

ROOF ADDITION PLAN

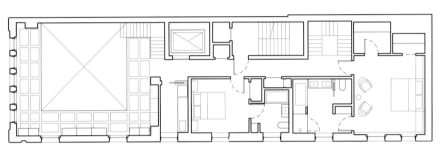

THIRD FLOOR PLAN

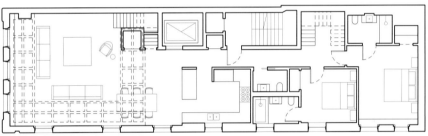

SECOND FLOOR PLAN

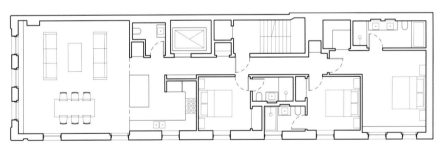

FIRST FLOOR PLAN

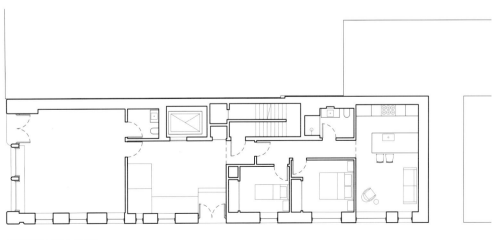

GROUND LEVEL PLAN

FACING PAGE TOP: Exposed brick walls lend a historic touch to the bedrooms.

FACING PAGE BOTTOM: The primary bathroom combines classic marble and fixtures with industrial details.

24

A steel and glass gallery is hung from the exposed beam ceiling in the living room.

FOLLOWING SPREAD: The addition on the roof, not visible to pedestrians on the street level, offers the apartment a direct connection to nature and the city beyond.

LOCATION	39 Lispenard Street, New York, NY
CLIENT	Undisclosed
SIZE	5,200 SF
TEAM	Eran Chen, Ryoko Okada, Kris Levine, Belen Pena, Christopher Sjoberg, Tulika Lokapur, Chris Pounds

TRIBECA LOFT

In a historic neighborhood like Tribeca, once one of New York's primary manufacturing districts, the deep industrial floor plates can present an exciting blank slate for a residential renovation, but simultaneously require a thoughtful approach to bringing in natural light and allowing a connection to the city outside its walls. Extending from Lispenard Street to Canal Street, this loft renovation is defined by an expansive living room framed by 50 feet of windows that brings in natural daylight.

To transform this century-old loft in Tribeca into a contemporary home for a family of five, we embraced the industrial character of the space and used open areas to give an airy feel. The design team restored the exposed beams and original columns that give the space its industrial feel, accented by exposed brick walls and blackened steel trim. The large industrial kitchen opens onto the great room. The centerpiece sofa offers seating on two sides, creating a 360-degree entertaining space, which also includes a 20-foot dining table.

The great room separates the public space from the private. Behind a series of panels, doors, and brick columns are an art gallery, home office, family room, and guest suite. Beyond that are the primary suite and three bedrooms for the children. And a Ketra lighting system allows light color temperature to track with daylight color to create a feeling of natural lighting within the space. The bedrooms open onto a 300-square-foot sunroom that runs parallel to Canal Street. The black-tiled space is filled with plants and acts as an urban green zone for the family to relax.

Entertaining is central to this open loft space, which is anchored by a 20-foot reclaimed wood dining table.

The expansive living and dining
spaces take advantage of the open
loft floor plate.

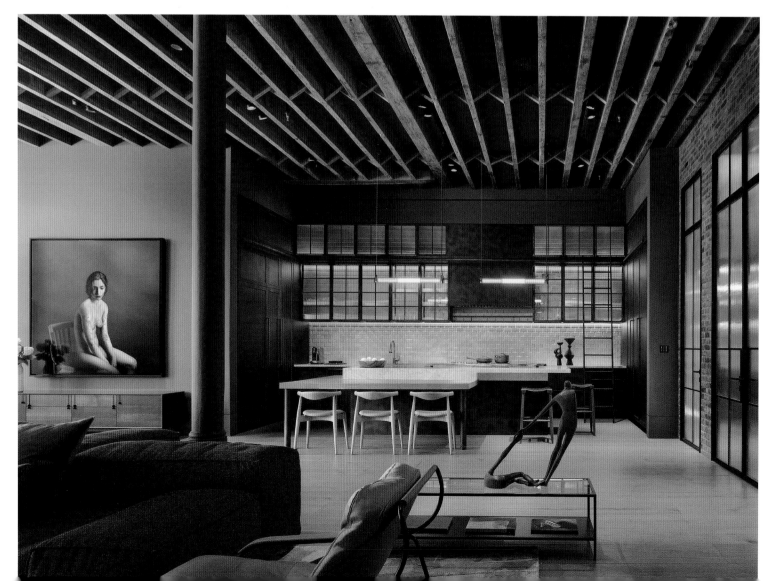

FLOOR PLAN

FACING PAGE: A material palette of
brick, steel, and glass nod to the
building's industrial past.

FOLLOWING SPREAD: The steel and
wood accents highlight both the
functional and decorative elements
of the space.

ABOVE: The primary suite is connected to the street through an indoor garden zone.

FACING PAGE: The primary bathroom offers a clean and contemporary setting.

FOLLOWING SPREAD: The four bedrooms open up to a sunroom garden space overlooking Canal Street.

BUILD

How can we extend the envelope-expanding approach I wrote about in the previous chapter to a greater scale to cultivate moments of beauty and connection and to further our vision for a new kind of city living that speaks to our emotions and that which makes us human?

The answer lies in what I call the "breathing room" of a building, the extent by which a building's envelope can expand and contract in order to discover new territories.

Expanding the envelope at the individual apartment level is all about reimagining quality of life in small private living spaces within big cities, with wider exposures to the streetscape below and more attention to the distinct experience of the "threshold." Now, with the bigger scale of an entire building, the task ahead is to leverage the breathing room of the overall structure, unlocking the buried potential for joy and human connection in all common areas, and ultimately bringing forth something that's greater than the sum of its parts.

But first we need to understand how we, as city dwellers, found ourselves in this strange predicament, living in extreme proximity with our neighbors but often feeling quite disconnected from them, from the street life below, as well as from the natural elements.

HOW WE GOT HERE

With the invention of the safety brake by Elisha Graves Otis in 1852 and the installation of the first commercial elevator in New York City in 1857, skylines of cities around the world soon shifted from horizontal arrangements of buildings to vertical ones. Not only were skyscrapers now a reality, but the new vertical approach had the effect of turning the most valuable real estate on its head, from the ground floor to the penthouse.

The legacy of that change is still with us today. The thinking is that by consolidating the infrastructure and amenities, and accommodating the functional needs of many people together, all in one place, we are able to not only meet the ever-increasing demand for urban housing but also do our part to provide affordable options and foster sustainability, reducing energy consumption and the need to travel for services.

This is a good, positive thing. Moreover, it is a necessity in a rapidly growing world that leaves less and less room for traditional horizontal architectural arrangements.

Prior to vertical consolidation, people lived on farms or in individual cabins and homesteads and such. (This was true even in a place like Manhattan that has been a high-density metropolis for centuries now.) But over time a dramatic horizontal consolidation transformed how we all live, bringing about the rise of not just urban rowhouses, townhouses, brownstones, and the like, but also the massive growth of suburbs. Across the board, this horizontal approach to building more homes involved reducing the amount of space between buildings or land (i.e., leaving less of a gap between).

Much was gained with the vertical consolidation that followed. Not only did it bring enormous efficiencies, but there was also the impressive height of the new structures and of course the great views.

But much was lost too: in building these towers in the sky, we got farther and farther from the street below, where the public realm exists. Unlike with horizontal consolidation, the new vertical dwellings lacked meaningful connection, visual and physical, to the land and streetscape. We crossed a threshold in urban development where a new level of density resulted in buildings that lack context. Missing, in particular, were all the ways in which one's personal life intersected with the life of the greater community.

Crossing this threshold radically changed the way we live. As architects, we were now designing at this new, bigger vertical scale, but we took our eyes off the ball (i.e., the context by which each of the apartment units related to the other units) to other people, to the streets, the landscape, the community. These buildings essentially became containers, for putting as many people as possible into one contiguous structure.

To put it another way, we used vertical consolidation as a multiplier. This gave us the ability to stack these boxes, these individual apartment units, atop one another to an almost exponential degree.

Duplicating individual apartment units vertically was necessary for accommodating the huge growth of cities—a mass transit for *housing*, if you will. And today we recognize that the enduring need to condense people in cities is more than a need; it's our responsibility to build this way, with an eye to sustainability and efficiencies in infrastructure and support.

We must keep the vertical model. There's no going back to how things were a century ago. But is there a way to think differently about vertical consolidation, and bring back to these structures some of the human, experiential qualities we lost along the way?

THE FOUR HUMAN DESIRES

In order to resolve this dilemma—and restore some of what we've had to sacrifice in our vertical consolidation—we need to look at four core human desires related to urban planning, city living, and architecture in general.

First is the desire to see far and beyond, to be in a place where you can actually understand your wider context. Second is the desire to live both inside and outside, to be able to immediately transition between the state of enclosure and that of being outdoors. Third is the desire to live with others and have a sense of community. Fourth is the desire to be shielded and protected, to have our own private space.

We need all four. But really, it's numbers two and three where we've paid the highest price by going vertical: we've lost the indoor/outdoor connection and the sense of community. So how can we find a way to accommodate these essential human impulses while we continue to consolidate vertically in the way we build?

We already discussed in the previous chapter the distinct qualities of outdoor terraces that have been given our envelope-expanding treatment, where the threshold itself is an experience and you feel like you're in when you're actually out. But beyond one's private balcony, how can we use this concept of the indoor-outdoor threshold and apply it to shared outdoor spaces for getting to know neighbors?

What other architectural platforms can we build so that people can connect and interact? Can the shared outdoor spaces be expanded to create new opportunities for communities to engage with one another? And can these buildings provide other *indoor* platforms that bring about the same threshold feeling we talked about in the individual apartment unit, that of an uncommitted, flexible space to engage with others?

The answer is yes. And the way to do it is by expanding the envelope.

LOCATION	15 Renwick Street, New York, NY
CLIENT	IGI-US
SIZE	70,000 SF
TEAM	Eran Chen, Ryoko Okada, P. Christian Bailey, Chris Berino, Come Menage, Kristina Kesler, Alonso Ayala, Abby Bullard

15 RENWICK

Space is at a premium in a dense city like New York, and privacy can often feel like a privilege. Designers often work to identify and optimize urban voids to create separation between neighbors and a sense of distance from the rest of the city. The design of 15 Renwick defines a broader threshold between exposure and seclusion, opportunity and intimacy.

At 15 Renwick, we split typical setback zoning requirements to create slices of green and outdoor space in the building's upper units. New York City's strict dormer rule, which asserts that only a certain amount of floor area may encroach into the setback line, often limits architectural design, but with this project, we saw this guideline as a launchpad for innovation. Manipulating the standard zoning dormer pyramid resulted in the discovery of spatial opportunity and a bolder link between indoor, outdoor, and semi-outdoor. A flying dormer structure is also employed, as opposed to columns, and can be seen from penthouse interiors.

A seamless union of steel, wood, and glass, 15 Renwick's facade is framed with dark aluminum reflective fins that, when touched by light, create shadow lines for recession and amplify privacy. When angled beneath the fins, pedestrians no longer have unrestricted views into private spaces. These unitized facade systems were prefabricated for each residence, brought to the site, and quickly, easily installed. The exterior's deep-set slim frames with wood-like inserts find renewed interpretation within the building, adding to its classic appeal and minimalistic details.

This project was the first in a long line of designs where we manipulated the standard zoning dormer pyramid, now a common practice within our office. Situated in Hudson Square, between SoHo and Tribeca, 15 Renwick explores the relationship between self and surrounding, all while harkening back to the neighborhood's bygone era of harbors, industrialization, and "the old neighborhood."

The building facade is composed of a series of individual frames, each serving as the facade of a physical window. At 4 feet by 8 feet, the frames maintain a human scale that break down the large scale of the building as a whole.

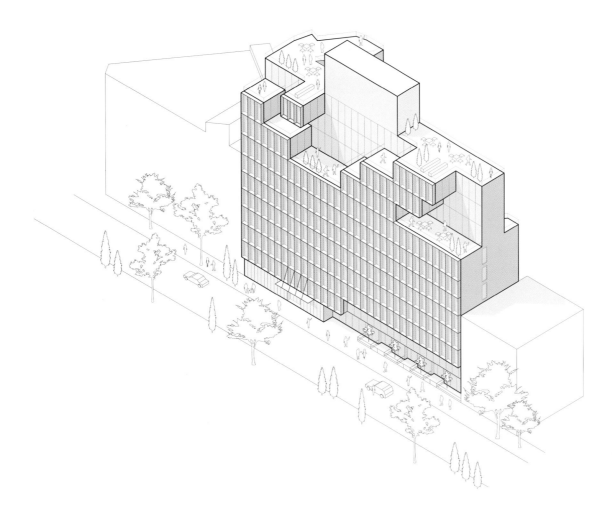

FACING PAGE: Upper level volumes
stagger across the facade while
keeping the grid of frames intact.

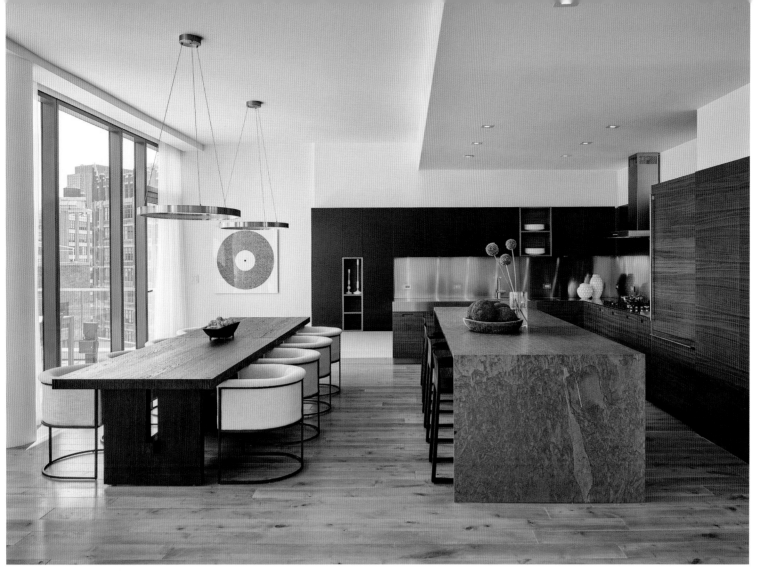

The staggered volumes create
unexpected views, moments
of connection between residents,
and pockets of outdoor space.

LOCATION	100 Norfolk, New York, NY
CLIENT	Adam America Real Estate
SIZE	49,900 SF
TEAM	Eran Chen, Ryoko Okada, P. Christian Bailey, Kris Levine, Kyriakos Kyriakou, Yaarit Sharoni, Karen Evans, Sharon Blaustein, Unjae Pyon

100 NORFOLK

A city's zoning regulations and building codes can quickly feel highly restrictive, dampening efforts to change the status quo. But we've often found that working within such prescriptions, Manhattan blocks can reveal unexpected urban possibilities. In a fluid give-and-take between the governing rules and development ambitions, 100 Norfolk takes the typical building model and flips it on its head, finding value in the sky.

Rather than growing vertically, 100 Norfolk grows diagonally, enjoying increments of area every two floors. Studying the adjacent properties revealed 11,000 square feet of available air rights that could be incorporated to the development. This redistribution of area had to happen under a strict zoning height limitation, forcing the volume to exploit its cantilevering potential. This maximized the area toward the top of the building and in consequence improved its efficiency. Sixty percent of the floor area at 100 Norfolk is located above the middle floor. The massing configuration increases the building's roof area, generating a top floor that boasts double the footprint of the ground floor. In addition, one of the roofs of the merged properties is integrated as an amenity terrace, offering tenants direct access to outdoor space.

While the cantilevers followed an efficiency logic, the concession of the light and air easement readdressed what was meant to be a naked party wall to the main facade of the building. Now the building turns as it grows, it is accessed from Norfolk Street, the elevator core is pushed far from Delancey's front, and the apartments surround it in a 180-degree setup. The building's direct translation of the reversed massing diagram is accomplished through a system of exposed structural trusses. This unconventional morphology is celebrated on the building skin, making it a form of identity and value. Through the advantageous utilization of building code and air rights, 100 Norfolk grows from an interior lot building to a corner lot icon.

While 100 Norfolk is located mid-block, the building turns as it grows toward the corner, allowing it two facades—one on Norfolk Street and one on Delancey Street.

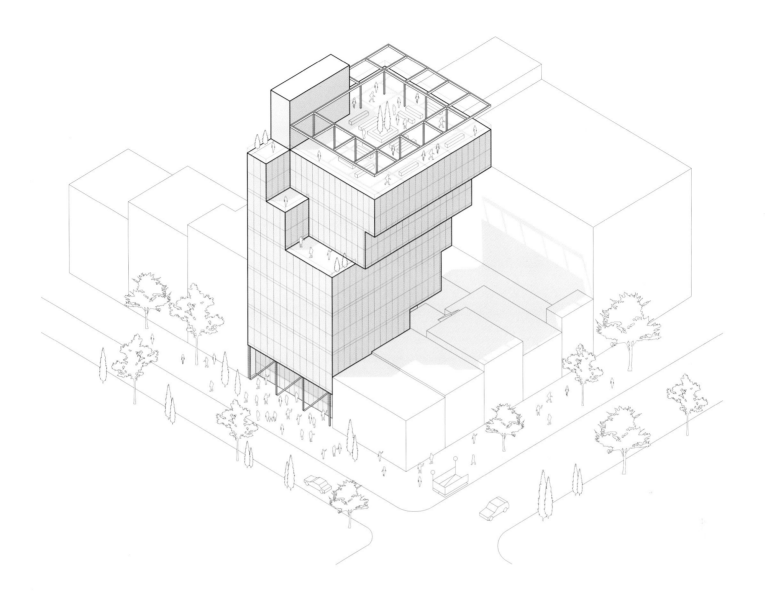

FACING PAGE: Rather than growing
vertically, 100 Norfolk expands
diagonally, with larger upper levels.

LOCATION	2222 Jackson Avenue, Long Island City, NY
CLIENT	Gershon Equities
SIZE	168,000 SF
TEAM	Eran Chen, Ryoko Okada, P. Christian Bailey, Kris Levine, Elizabeth Snow, Keith Burns, Karen Evans, Carolina Moscoso

2222 JACKSON

In architecture, flexibility and adaptability create opportunity. Breaking out of the box, freeing oneself from the mold, can inspire new possibilities, but what if that box is where real opportunity is found? At 2222 Jackson Avenue in Long Island City, that notion is manifested with a modular design that yields dynamic residential experiences.

The mobility of the street wall at 2222 Jackson, which had the potential to live as much as 10 feet away from the street itself, stirred ideas of inclusions and extrusions. Divided into a modulated grid of 12 feet by which all structural and building systems are stacked, the site functions as a matrix with three apartment typologies: studios with one bay, one-bedrooms with two bays, and two-bedrooms with three bays. The studios are longer than their one- and two-bedroom counterparts and project seven feet beyond the facade, dancing along the face of the building, creating corner windows for apartments above. During construction the push and pull of exterior lines provided unparalleled flexibility in layout, while post-construction it resulted in 50 terraced apartments and a vertical city with 30 percent more outdoor space than the footprint of the building itself.

Following creative cues from the nearby MoMA PS1, 2222 Jackson boasts a concrete facade to complement the aesthetic identity of its notable neighbor. By understanding the resilience of design, layout, and material, and through the findings made at a previous project, 2222 Jackson Avenue uncovered a simple, tectonic way to unite innovation with efficiency without sacrificing a commitment to the vertical village.

With its dynamic facade, 2222 Jackson was designed to attract people to live in the post-industrial neighborhood of Long Island City.

By setting the entire building back
from the street, bays can be projected
beyond the facade line to create a
playful composition.

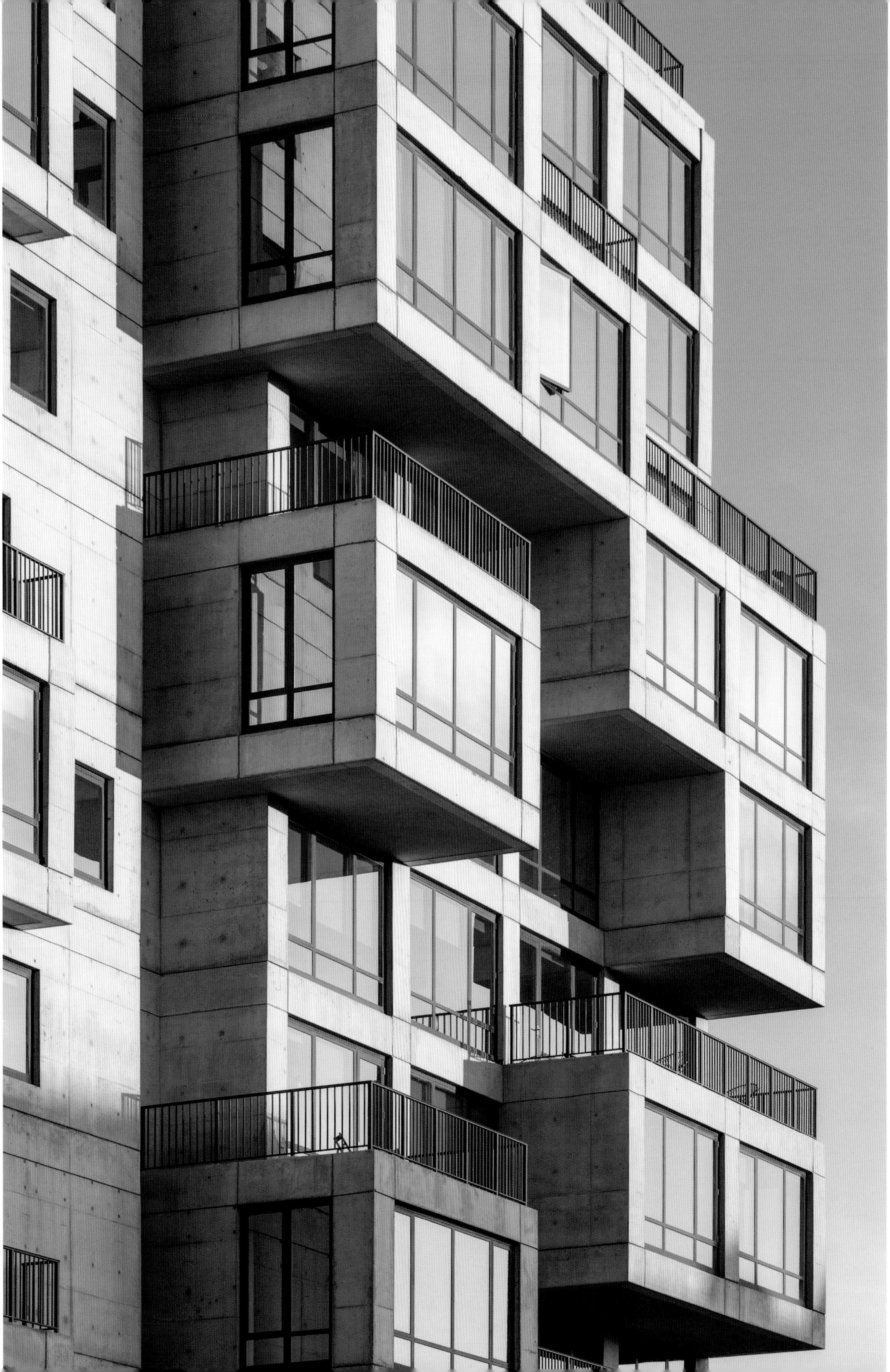

FACING PAGE: Projected bays create
sizable terraces distributed across
the facade.

LOCATION	251 First Street, Brooklyn, NY
CLIENT	Adam America Real Estate
SIZE	80,000 SF
TEAM	Eran Chen, Ryoko Okada, P. Christian Bailey, Dongyoung Kim, Vi Nguyen, Hadas Brayer, Asuncion Tapia

251 FIRST STREET

New York's strict urban grid has lent the city its efficiency but amplifies the contrast between bustling avenues and quiet residential streets. Corner lots are left to straddle the two characters, often forced to privilege one over the other. At the crossroads of Fourth Avenue and First Street, the twisted geometry of 251 First Street celebrates the corner's transition from busy main avenue to residential side street, rich with landmarked brownstones. In the building's dissipating facade, both characters collide.

The building's mass expresses both large-scale neighborhood changes and a feeling of intimacy. The sensory experiences in and around 251 First Street are more natural for residents and neighbors, free of rigid corners and hard edges, replaced with soft lines and exposed space. The series of bars in the windows that sprawl along the avenue create proportions suited for its retail environment, a far cry from the recessed, terraced look of First Street's facade.

The fragmentation of terraces carries the social life of the streetscape up and into the building.

The stepped back corner offers a
moment of transition from the busy
avenue to the quiet street.

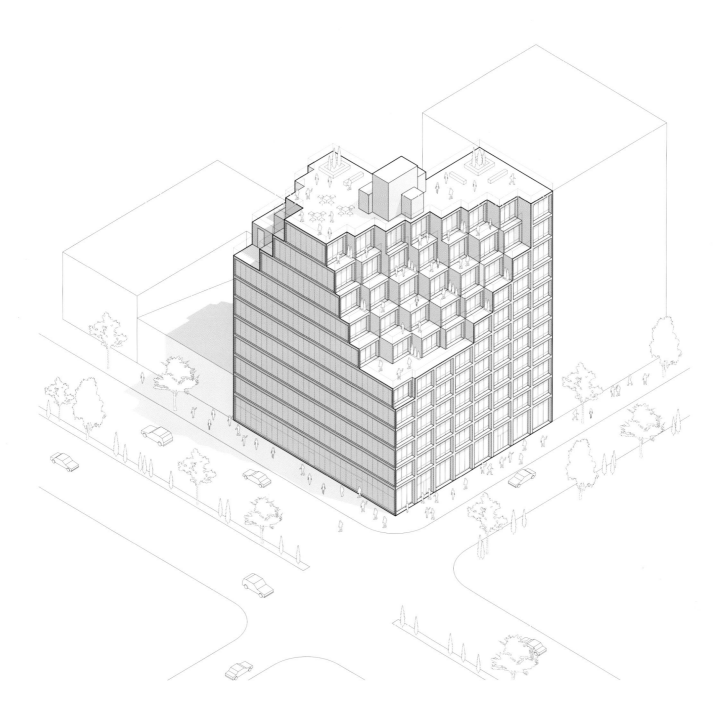

FACING PAGE: The interiors emphasize
natural materials and rich textures.

LOCATION	10 Jay Street, Brooklyn, NY
CLIENT	Triangle Assets, Glacier Global Partners
SIZE	179,900 SF
TEAM	Eran Chen, Ryoko Okada, P. Christian Bailey, Dongyoung Kim, Mark Bearak, Carolina Moscoso, Kate Samuels, Yongchun Choi, Unjae Pyon

10 JAY

As cities densify and run out of buildable land, adaptive reuse is an increasingly necessary practice. 10 Jay Street is a prime example of how we can recover buildings for new use. Its design creates tangible threads to link old with new; the industrial age with the digital era; distinction and synthesis. At 10 Jay, a vanished facade has prompted a reflection on the present and a look back to industrial history.

On Dumbo's waterfront in Brooklyn, flanked by the Manhattan Bridge and flush with East River views, integrating new design with the site's landmark heritage was more than a creative vision, it was a developmental demand. 10 Jay Street honors the relationship between the neighborhood and water's edge, heritage, and innovation. A delicate balance of glass, steel, brick, and spandrels give the building gravitas without compromising its industrial heritage.

Constructed in 1898, the Arbuckle Brothers Sugar Refinery was composed of two steel frame buildings with brick curtain walls, set parallel to the river with a shared interior facade. When the river-facing factory building was demolished in the 1950s, the interior party wall was left exposed to the East River shore. Our design team dug into the site's history, drawing a series of new skins that evoked sugar crystals and reflected its proximity to the water. Our exterior intervention reclaims the fracture between the two buildings and has made this part of the narrative: a broken geode smooth on the outside and crystalline within. With its facets, the new facade also speaks to the park and the river, the sunset, the Manhattan Bridge rising beside it, the riverfront on the other side, and the sugar originally processed on the site.

As the conversation surrounding heritage and preservation grows, 10 Jay Street challenges the way we view history. The facade and the building's interior received fifteen permits from New York City's Landmarks Preservation Commission, which often holds jewel-box designs to intense scrutiny. One of the permits noted that the design is "in keeping with the utilitarian character of the building."

By weaving the historic narrative of the building and its use into the design for the new facade, the building is transformed into a structure with continued relevance—a reflection of the past, present, and future of this notable part of the city.

The late nineteenth-century facade was preserved and renovated to highlight its industrial heritage.

What was once a hidden facade, now faces the Brooklyn waterfront, and shapes the view from Manhattan.

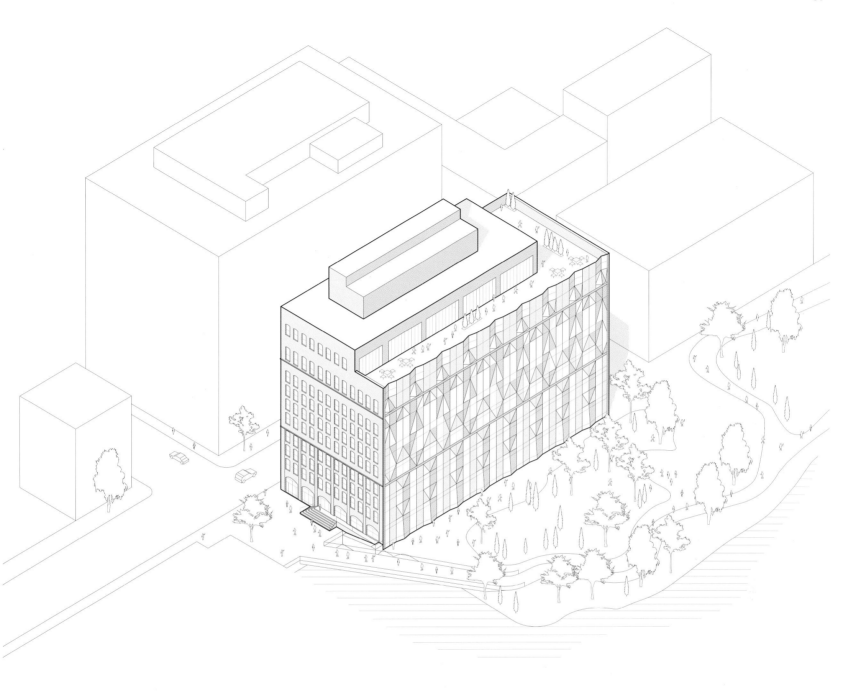

New elements meet the old structure,
celebrating the palimpsests of the city.

At night, the faceted facade shimmers
like the nearby river.

LOCATION	1040 Dean Street, Brooklyn, NY
CLIENT	All Year Management
SIZE	133,325 SF
TEAM	Eran Chen, Ryoko Okada, P. Christian Bailey, Francois Blehaut, Zac Zeller, Come Menage, Kristina Kesler, Alonso Ayala

1040 DEAN

Adjacent to the former Nassau Brewery complex, 1040 Dean Street's industrial facade honors the history of its 150-year-old neighbor. Inside the eight-story building, an industrial material palette of wood, concrete, and steel extends into the amenity spaces, including a social space with pool tables, lounge areas, and stepped seating.

Rental units are arranged around the L-shaped building. Toward the interior of the block, balconies overlook a landscaped internal courtyard, which carves out spaces for residents to connect not only on the ground level, but vertically with their neighbors. The building includes large rooftop terraces with spaces for lounging, dining, and gathering, and with views back to Manhattan.

The interior of the block becomes a lush communal garden.

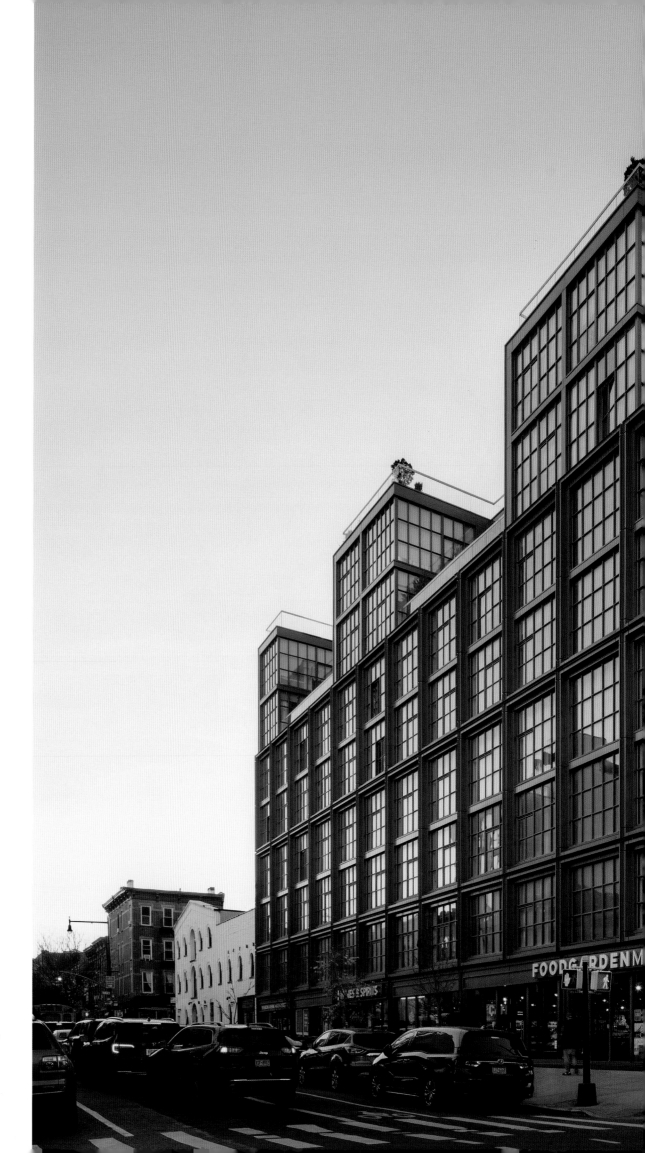

The facade of the L-shaped building is broken up through smaller framing, reducing its scale and presenting a more pedestrian-friendly experience to engage the street.

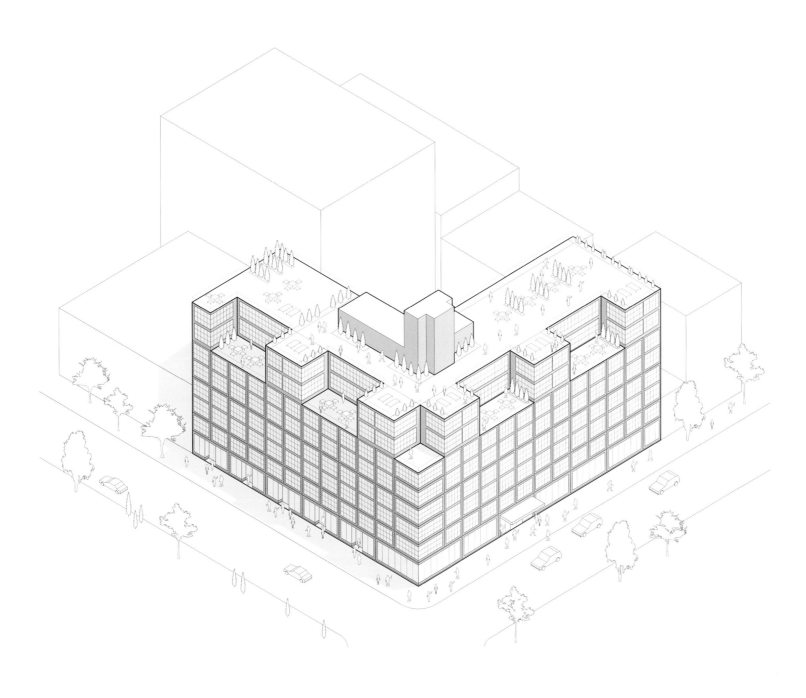

FACING PAGE: Balconies overlook the landscaped courtyard.

FOLLOWING SPREAD: The building offers a number of communal spaces where residents can connect.

LOCATION	42-20 27th Street, Queens, NY
CLIENT	The Rabsky Group
SIZE	192,000 SF
TEAM	Eran Chen, P. Christian Bailey, Dongyoung Kim, Soo Bum You, Francesco Asaro, Philip Jenkins, Sejung Kim, Sudarshan Venkatraman, Lilia Sodre

BEVEL

In the rapidly developing residential area of Long Island City, where most of the building stock consists of newly constructed high-rises, how can we carve out authentic moments that celebrate street culture? In Bevel, a shifted mass and lifted facade opens up opportunities for unexpected pockets of social interaction between tenants and pedestrians, inner courtyards and gardens, and oversized terraces.

Bevel pairs concrete and glass to form an 85-foot atrium in the heart of the building. From there, the stepped facade creates a "beveled" shape, allowing more than half of the units to have large private outdoor spaces, either looking out to the New York skyline, or inward to the building's botanical gardens.

The atrium boasts a display of public art, the successor of our collaboration with local art nonprofit, the Bushwick Collective, at Denizen in Bushwick. For Bevel, the Bushwick Collective selected artist Dalek to design and paint the space. Dalek's mural peeks through the lobby, engaging both residents and passersby outside of the building.

At the base of the building, the cutouts' voids allow for a transfer of FAR to the top of the building, enabling us to create the stepped facade, moving units higher up for better views as well as additional private outdoor space that would not be available within a typical building massing.

Two botanical gardens, one 65 feet and the other 75 feet high, have openings to the exterior, forming a visible connection to pedestrians in the neighborhood. We also included a lush courtyard as an outdoor oasis, replete with greenery and lounge furniture. The tranquil ambiance is enhanced by energy efficient windows that block out the noise of the city, a graceful water feature, and supple green walls.

The lifted corner reveals a deep look into the building, and lends the structure its name.

The ground-level lobby spaces connect
to the street visually.

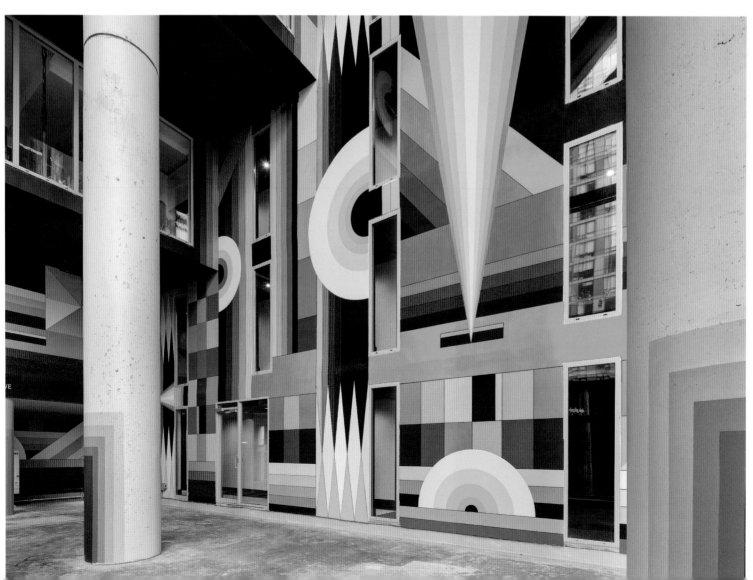

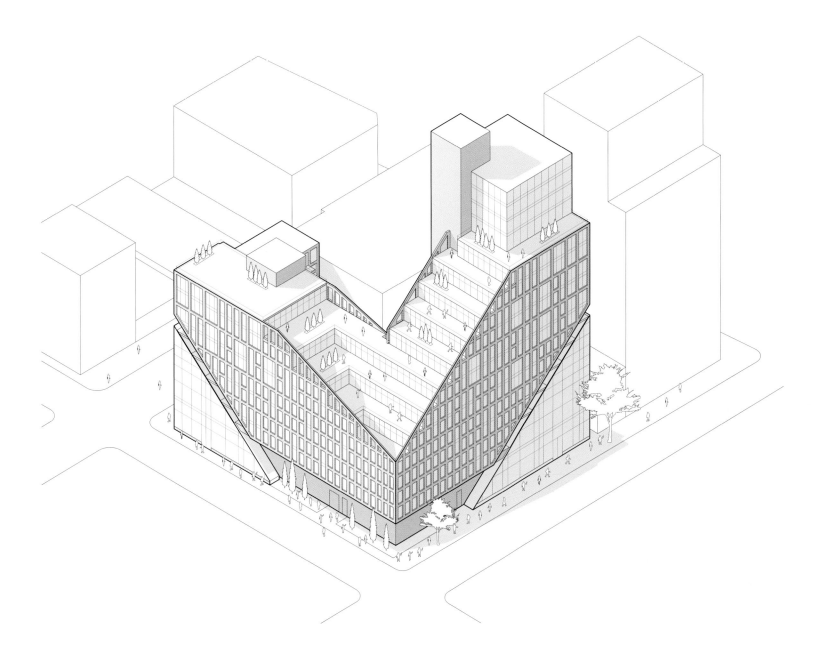

ABOVE: The interiors, by Durukan Design, complement the exterior and architecture with industrial materials and a pop of color.

FACING PAGE: A water feature adds an earthy feel to the large concrete columns in the residents' lounge.

LOCATION	212 West 93rd Street, New York, NY
CLIENT	Landsea and Leyton
SIZE	65,000 SF
TEAM	Eran Chen, Gene Pyo, Kyriakos Kyriakou, Bernhard Stocker, Francois Blehaut, Shin-Yau Huang, Patricia Gortari, Brona Waldron, Boram Lee Jung, Jennifer Endozo, Seung Bum Ma, Ivan Heredia, Adrienne Milner, Francesco Asaro, Jason Bourgeois, Karen Evans, Soo Bum Kim

212 WEST 93RD

Sitting above a synagogue, 212 West 93rd Street builds upon the sense of community that is inherent in a religious gathering space. ODA designed the massing to pull in and out, creating oversized terraces for each of the building's 20 condo units, encouraging interaction between neighbors. Natural light plays a big role in the building's positioning—the floor plans, as well as the location of the projecting bay windows and oversized terraces, are based on the building's exposure to sunlight. The rhythm of projections and setbacks create intimate moments of surprise and discovery throughout the building. Envisioned as an extension of Central Park, 212 West 93rd Street emphasizes a strong connection between indoor and out.

Residents of Landsea and Leyton's 60,000 SF, boutique 20-unit condo will enjoy ample outdoor space, connection to nature and amazing lighting. The exclusive number of units allows for maximum outdoor space per condo, as well as views of the area and Central Park.

Rather than a traditional setback, the building's facade pushes in and out for a dynamic overall massing.

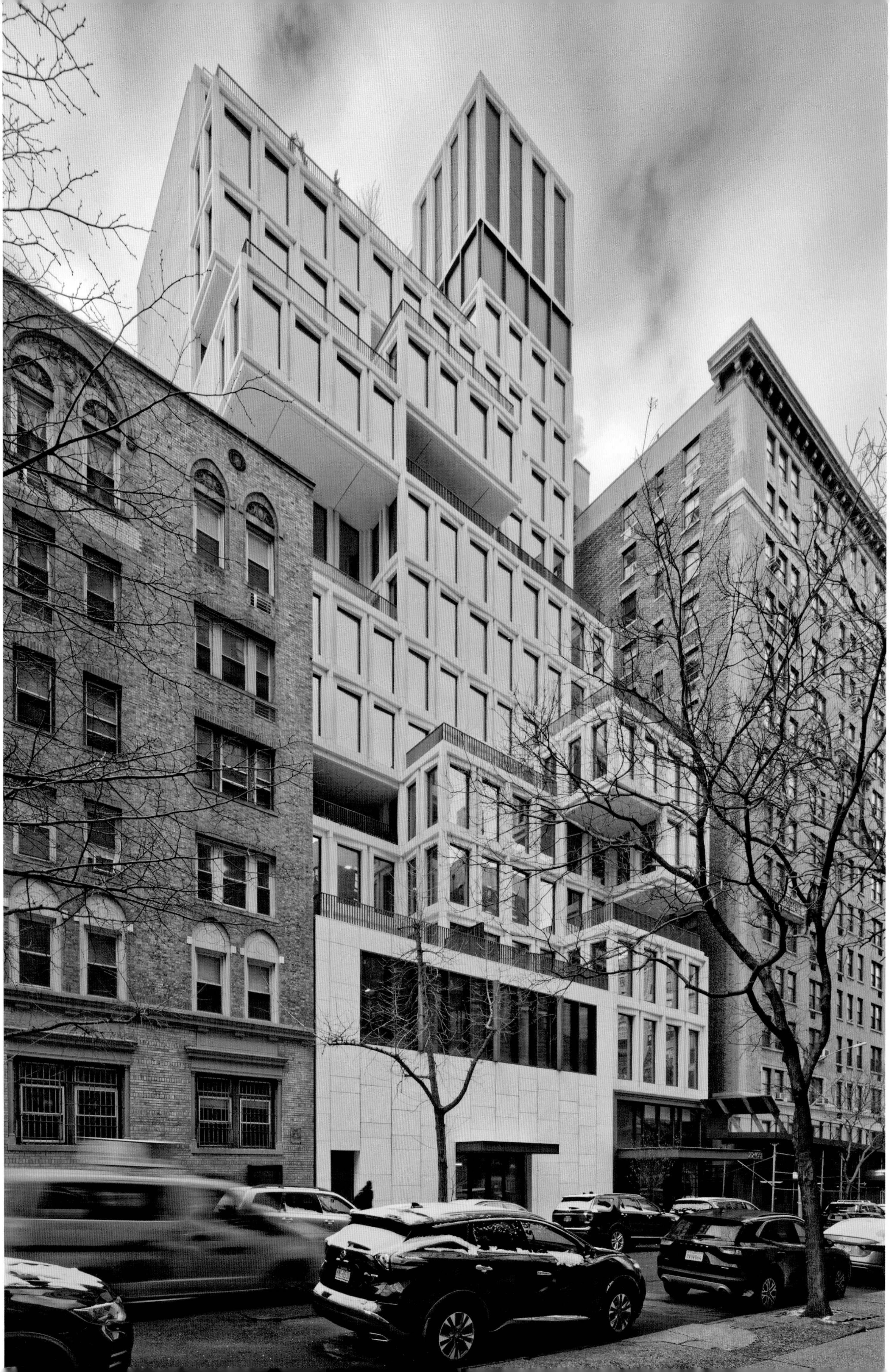

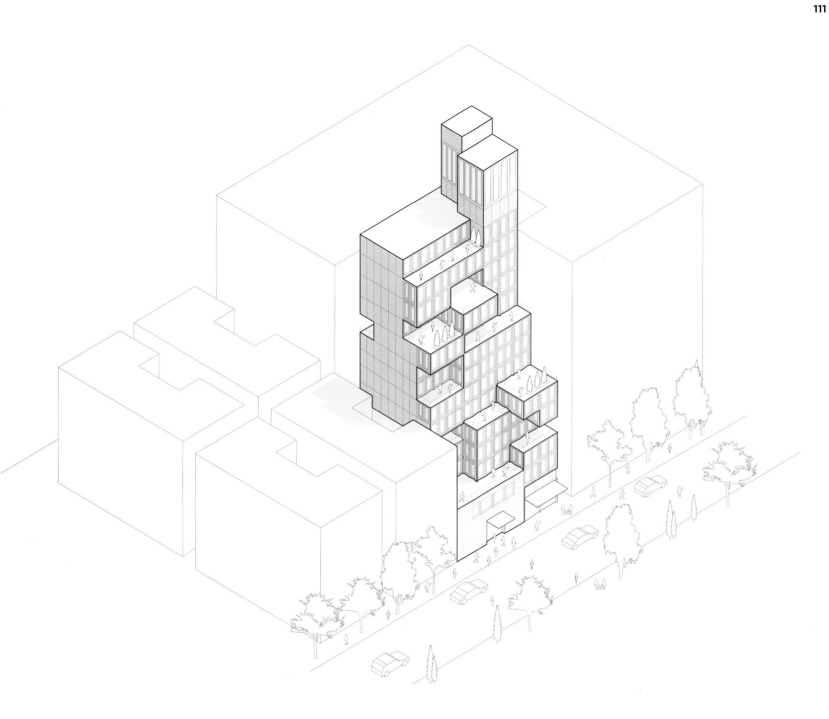

FACING PAGE: Re-imagined bay windows bring staggered terraces to the traditional context of the Upper West Side.

LOCATION	2505 Broadway, New York, NY
CLIENT	Adam America Real Estate
SIZE	106,445 SF
TEAM	Eran Chen, Olivera Grk, Ryoko Okada, Kris Levine, Christopher Sjoberg, Jessica Schoen, Belen Pena, Matthew Boker, Mohammad Askarzadeh, Saranya Kanagaraj, Pablo Zapeda, Jacob Hedaya, Adi Krainer

2505 BROADWAY

Manhattan's Upper West Side is one of New York's longest standing, iconic neighborhoods, and 2505 Broadway seeks to complement this heritage in its neighborhood-scale, timeless materiality, and elegant proportions.

2505 Broadway's design is a modern take on the traditional architecture of the Upper West Side, embracing the hallmarks of classic prewar buildings. Most of the area's architecture is made exclusively of brick masonry. The design uses this same material to create the building's facade to weave it into the fabric of the neighborhood. The 19-story building aims to elevate the area's classic heritage with custom, curved Petersen bricks, whose hand-molded fabrication in Denmark by eighth-generation brickmakers creates a richness in texture and character. The facade's rounded, vertical piers rise from the street level and taper into terraced setbacks at the top of the building.

The facade, private terraces, entrance foyers in the apartments, and details further embrace the trademarks of classic prewar buildings, while diverse floor plans, elevated amenities, and expanded outdoor spaces are tailored for contemporary residents.

2505 Broadway was designed from the outside in. Each of the building's residences is filled with natural light through oversized windows with historically inspired mullions that contrast the rich character of the masonry by adding crisp lines to the facade. Inside, marble, oak, and brass finishes were chosen to reinforce classical architectural elements. Every residence has access to the amenity rooftop terrace while select residences can also enjoy private balconies or their own private "backyards."

The classic masonry facade blends with the neighborhood's historic style, while the massing and oversized terraces mark the building as contemporary.

Elongated frames lend an elegant
verticality to the facade.

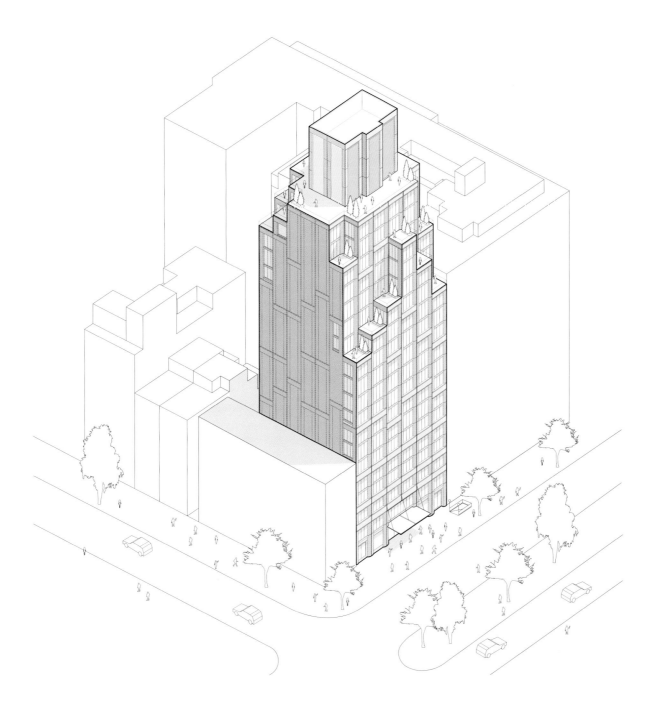

FACING PAGE: Overlooking Broadway
on 93rd Street, 2505 Broadway's
facade opens up, allowing interaction
with the city life.

The communal interiors pick
up on the classic Upper West Side
material palette, with a fresh and
contemporary edge.

A neutral material palette and thoughtfully placed details define the timeless residential interiors.

FOLLOWING SPREAD: Handmade curved brick creates elegant piers along the building's facade and delicately accentuates the use of classic masonry.

LOCATION	561 Pacific Street, Brooklyn, NY
CLIENT	Adam America Real Estate
SIZE	110,600 SF
TEAM	Eran Chen, Ryoko Okada, P. Christian Bailey, Kris Levine, Soo Bum You, Audrey Topp, Ruomei Zhang, Paul Kim, Dawoon Jung, Unjae Pyon, Emma Pfeiffer, Ascuncion Tapia, Chia-Min Wang, Tulika Lokapur

561 PACIFIC

Brooklyn's Boerum Hill neighborhood is characterized by tree-lined blocks and rows of historic brownstones. The natural elements and warm colors of the area serve as a starting point for the design of this new construction. The building's nearly hidden entrance is clad in wooden slats, and gives way to an intimate and inviting interior for the residents.

The building's interiors draw on the Japanese concept of wabi-sabi, which celebrates what is naturally incomplete. The wood, stone, concrete, and steel found throughout the interiors all have knots and grains with subtle imperfections, some of which will also change over time. Ivy also grows on the green wall just inside the lobby and up the amenity courtyard stairs, adding to the living elements of the building.

Three floors of amenities allow residents to relax and socialize. A private fitness center, children's playroom, and residents' lounge open onto a light-filled courtyard, and a communal roof deck offers further access to the outside.

A playful mix of window sizes throughout the facade draw interest in from the busy streets in Boerum Hill.

Japanese inspired details create an intimate entry into the building.

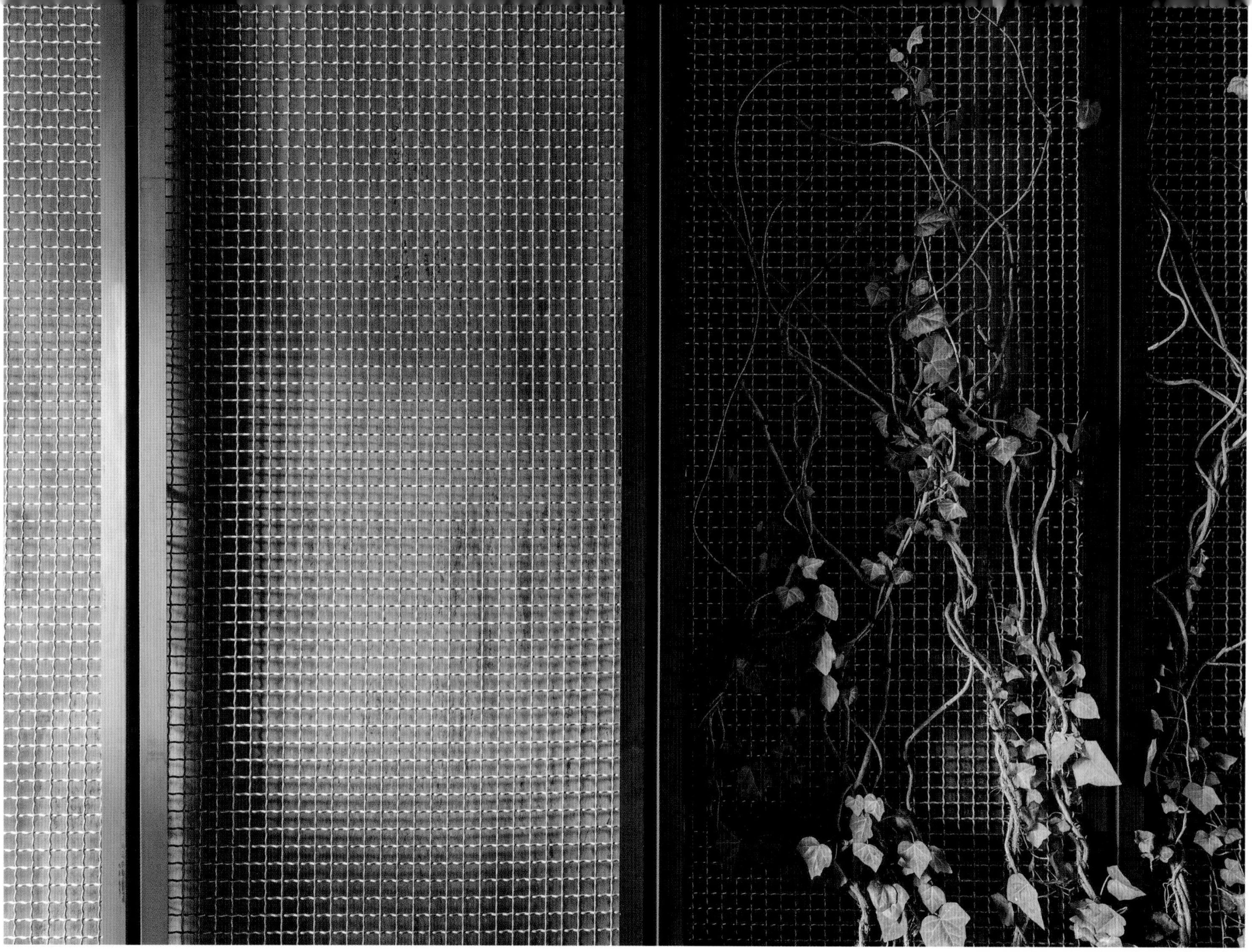

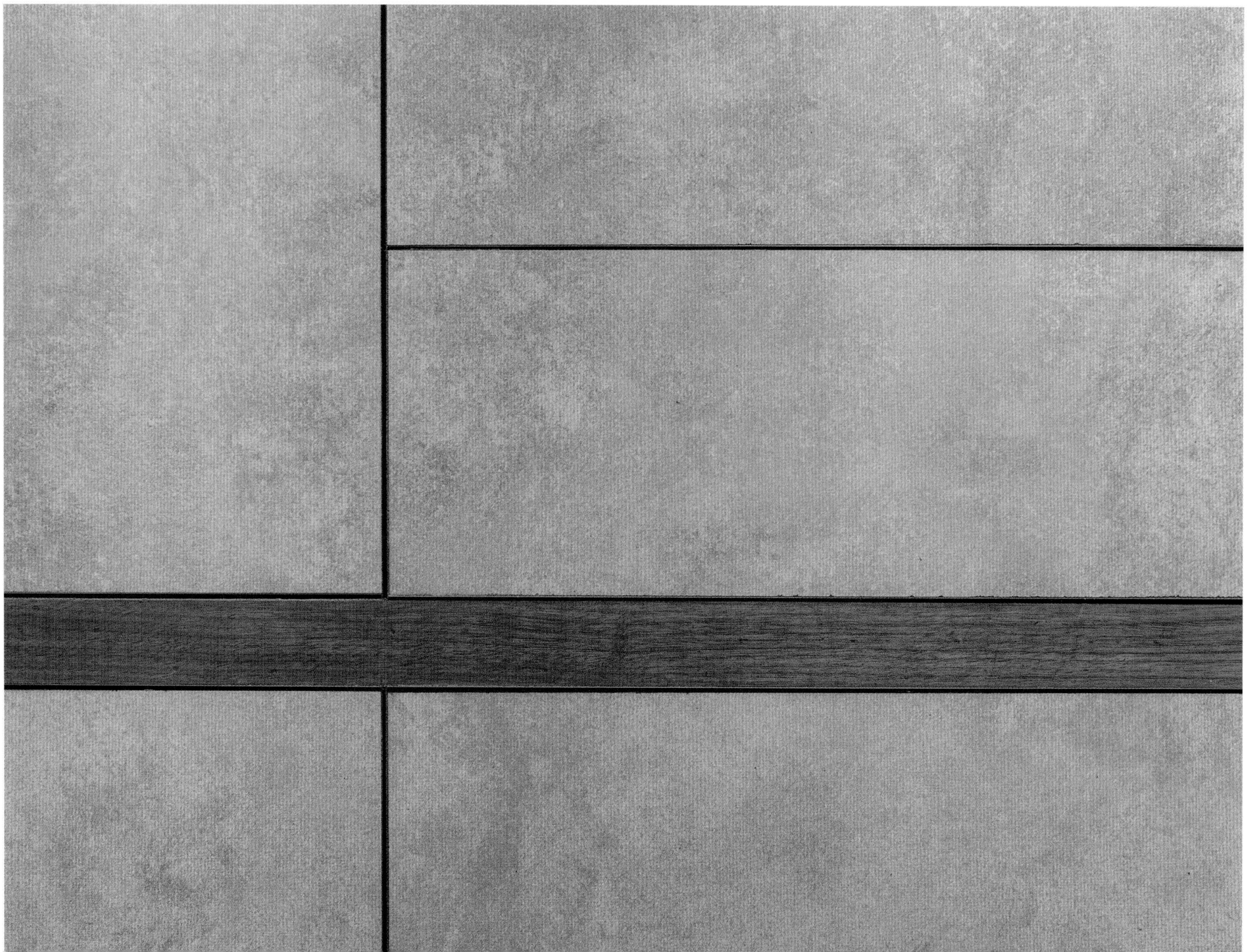

FACING PAGE: A natural and tactile
selection of materials defines the
interior.

A living and growing wall of ivy climbs through the lobby into the interior courtyard space, creating a visual connection and sense of transparency from the inside out.

LOCATION	101 West 14th Street, New York, NY
CLIENT	Gemini Rosemont
SIZE	82,776 SF
TEAM	Eran Chen, Bernhard Stocker, Chris Berino, Brian Lee, Olivera Grk, Arta Perezic, Taesoo Kim

101 WEST 14TH STREET

For many New Yorkers, 14th Street is the invisible border between downtown and the rest of the city. At this busy thoroughfare in the heart of the city, the repeating fractal pattern of the facade at 101 West 14th Street is intended to create space and breathing room. Its glass windows mark the corner with a sense of lightness and depth.

Here, quality of life is not measured in floor area, but in volume. The units have double-height living rooms that create a new perspective and movement through the space. Looking at the surroundings through the lens of floor-to-ceiling glass windows allows quiet and privacy but also a gradual indoor-to-outdoor experience. The apartments feature terraces so residents can connect directly to the city around them. At the interior of the building, garden apartments face an inner courtyard.

Operable 18-foot glass window panels create dramatic double height views and establish a connection with the busy street life at the corner of 14th Street and 6th Avenue.

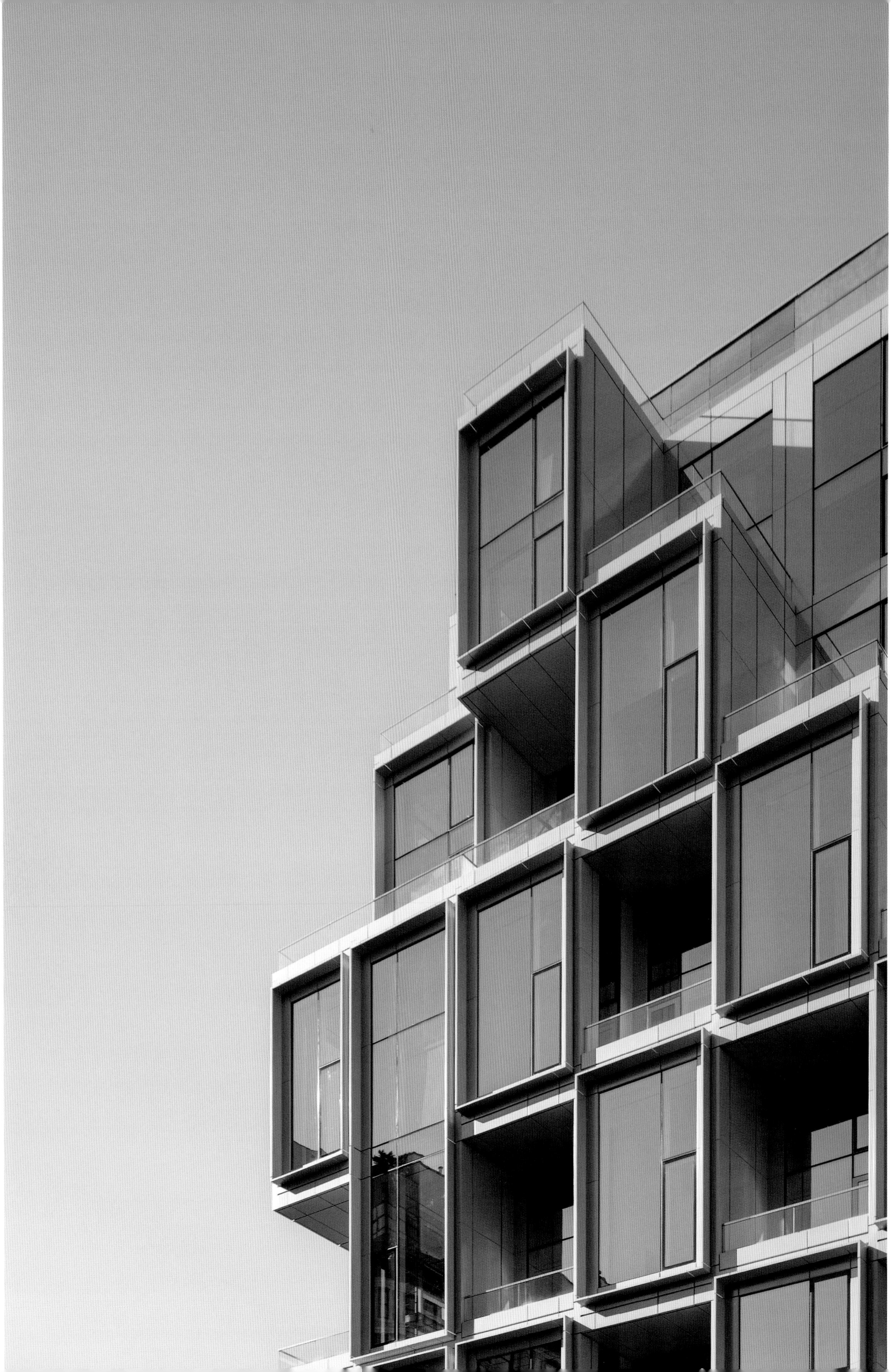

A unique and playful massing allows
for oversized terraces that interlock
throughout the building.

LOCATION	98 Front Street, Brooklyn, NY
CLIENT	Hope Street Capital
SIZE	189,000 SF
TEAM	Eran Chen, Kyriaokos Kyriakou, Patricia Gortari, Kris Levine, Jennifer Endozo, Dawoon Jung, Soo Bum, Jason Bourgeois, Karen Evans, Zac Zeller, Adrienne Milner, Yoonah Choi

98 FRONT

98 Front is the end-product of a study we conducted relating to what we refer to as the "breathing room" of a building—the degree to which it can expand and contract within the limitations of the zoning envelope. The intention was to explore the uncharted opportunities in a community of small dwelling units in dense cities. What seems complicated is in fact a very simple structure, designed from the inside-out.

Every unit is made of one to four modules, from a studio apartment to a three-bedroom home where the living room is always longer and projected beyond the base building line, just enough to allow it to have a corner window and an access to a large, furnishable terrace. This terrace is in fact the roof of another extended living room below. The result is a building where almost every apartment has more than one exposure to light and air and a large outdoor space expanding the indoor living-room experience.

Amenities are traditionally thought of as a series of rooms accommodating a long list of dedicated activities from different sports to study rooms and playrooms. For us, it's about the quality of those common areas, and how they can become an expansion of one's home. They must have natural light and air and arrange as open casual spaces that allow people to enjoy spontaneously, without prescribed purpose or a goal. At 98 Front, the common spaces within the building are placed on the street level and feel like an extension of the visible surroundings. They open up to an internal courtyard full of light. They have casual seating arrangements and dining tables and can be used as people wish.

The building is designed to echo the industrial history of Dumbo, which, to this day, is full of old warehouses and manufacturing buildings. Many of the neighborhood's buildings were built of concrete grid-like structures that maximized the load and open space of the floor plan. We used wood both inside and out to balance the concrete material, a lesson we learned from Louis Kahn. The underside of the cantilever is clad in wood panels that is experienced both from inside the apartments and from the street looking up. At night the light from the homes reflects on the wood surfaces, and glows with a deep haze.

The facade and structure of 98 Front pick up on Dumbo's industrial past, while contemporary elements lend it a sense of understated luxury.

Smaller cantilevers clad with an underside of wood give the building a sense of warmth and welcoming.

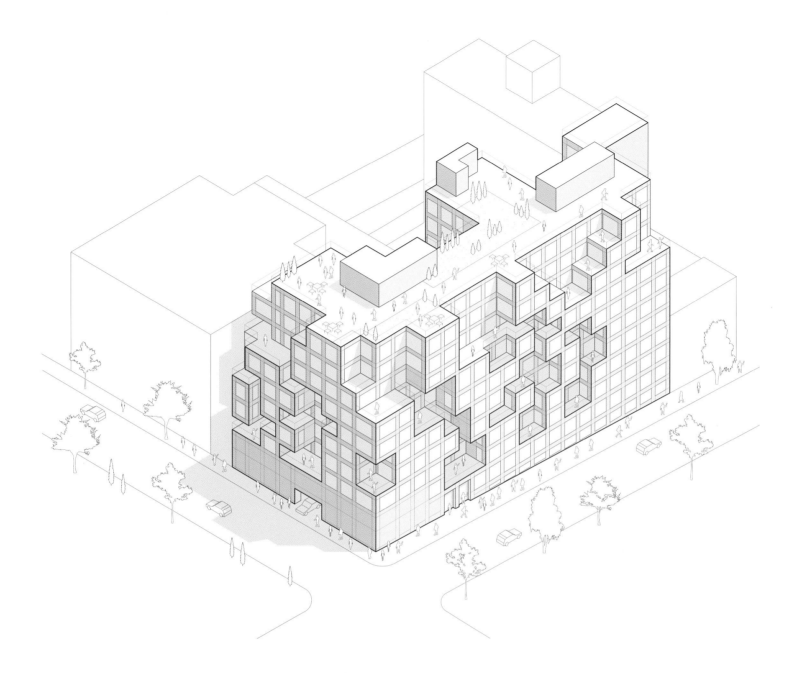

FACING PAGE TOP: Ground floor units open up into private interior courtyard spaces, serving as a backyard in a neighborhood with limited outdoor space.

BOTTOM LEFT: The industrial materiality of the facade continues into the interior of the units with exposed concrete ceilings.

BOTTOM RIGHT: Garden units have detached spaces inspired by the traditional carriage house, perfect for a home office space or entertaining.

Communal amenities offer social connection between residents.

BLOCK

et's Go Nats!
Hamilton
GATSBY
GATSBY
GATSBY
GATSBY
BASEBOWL
ENVY

What does expanding the envelope mean in the context of a full city block? The answer runs through many of the same concepts we've already discussed: the breathing room of the block, the potential for magical moments of discovery, the unique experience of the threshold, and the attention to oft-overlooked elements of emotion, humanity, and community.

In the same way we advocated for a new approach to vertical consolidation that opened up a building's envelope and uncovered hidden possibilities for joy and connection, now we look at the vertical relationships *between* buildings on a city block—and how we can use spaces like courtyards, plazas, and sidewalks to not only tie together disparate architectural projects and structures but also reimagine how people on the block relate to one another and to their environment.

A typical city block is made up of a number of individual properties, usually side by side, that are independently designed and constructed. Each building stands on its own. Typically, the only thing binding them together is the zoning code for the particular area or neighborhood. In New York City, these regulations are very general. Originally introduced in 1916, they've been updated periodically over the past century but mostly just involve rules related to maximum height and bulk, as well as setbacks from the street front or street wall.

New York's zoning guidelines are primarily meant to protect city dwellers' access to natural light and air, so that one building doesn't block exposure to these elements for another building, or for the street itself. The regulations don't attempt to control or influence the style of architectural design of the buildings. And they certainly don't take into consideration any kind of poetic beauty in the way the different buildings "talk" to one another.

BUILDINGS THAT TALK TO ONE ANOTHER

Mostly, what these basic zoning rules have done is just unite certain volumetric standards for individual buildings, imposing limits on what we call the "sweater" (or maximum bulk) of each. They don't create a dialogue between the different buildings on a given city block. And this is arguably a missed opportunity, because when buildings talk to one another, there's so much more to be gained.

Take, for example, our Parcel 8 at the Wharf project in Washington, D.C., where we built two distinct buildings—one a hotel, one private residences—but united them by making them part of the same single structure. One side climbs to form the residential building while the other side recedes to establish the hotel. This creates a clear visual delineation but also an appealing, complementary relationship between the two.

And that's only part of the story. When we built our structure, there was already an office building on one side and a high-end condo on the other, both designed by others. We could have just ignored our existing neighbors on the block but instead we did a full analysis, looking at the bigger picture of how our design for Parcel 8 would relate to these surrounding buildings. Ultimately, we shaped ours in a way that left an unusual amount of space between us and the two adjacent structures and opened up attractive view corridors toward the waterfront (the Wharf abuts the Potomac River in D.C.'s southwest riverfront neighborhood).

We also took into consideration the public space underneath, with a courtyard design visible from the street level that visually overlaps with the nearby park, bringing a sense of unity between Parcel 8 and its urban context. Finally, we created our own exciting ground floor that expanded the public realm, activating the main pedestrian path and welcoming street life into the ground program's restaurants and shops.

All in all, we built in a way that created a pleasing illusion that the different buildings and elements on this one city block had been talking to one another from the get-go.

This is what it looks like when you leverage the breathing room of a whole block to bring forth something greater than the sum of its parts.

But it's not necessarily easy to pull off. Not only do you have the zoning requirements that limit you to certain formulations, and of course your own program and business case that you need to satisfy; you have to build in a way that dances around all of this *and* accounts for your neighbors on the block, as well as the whole ground floor context, including sidewalks, streets, and parks.

It's worth the effort. For one thing, buildings that contribute to their block in a meaningful way tend to be more attractive to their occupants. They also foster a greater sense of community.

THE COMMUNITY OF A CITY BLOCK

This concept of community drives our envelope-expanding approach at every scale but becomes especially important when we get to the level of the city block. That's where we take ourselves out of our individual apartment unit and even beyond the secondary ring of social interaction we encounter when we connect with neighbors in our apartment building.

When we talk about a full city block, the whole experience becomes much more interactive, bringing with it a welcome opportunity to expand our engagement with people who aren't in our immediate circles.

Expanding the envelope at this bigger scale is also about the ability to bring more typologies into a city block, with residential buildings, hotels, offices, and more. This kind of mix is essential to creating vibrant mixed-use neighborhoods (as we'll see later in Chapter Four). And when it all comes together, like on the one waterfront block in D.C., it instills a richness that impacts residents and non-residents alike.

In the pages ahead, we'll explore a number of examples where we as an architectural firm had the chance to look in this way at an entire city block. In most cases, unlike with Parcel 8, we were fortunate to control the whole block and orchestrate the whole symphony, so to speak, from scratch. In fact, with our massive Denizen project in Brooklyn's Bushwick neighborhood, we controlled not one but two city blocks. While New York City's basic zoning requirements don't require any of this, we took the unusual step of asking the city to de-map the streets uniting those two blocks to make room for a public park and then a series of six city courtyards.

City-block courtyards are key to our approach with Denizen and elsewhere. These account for a huge slice of the overall open outdoor space in New York City. But they tend to be heavily underutilized and underpopulated.

In Bushwick, the sheer scale of our project—one million square feet of apartment units—gave us an unprecedented opportunity to look very closely at the typology of a typical New York City block and then apply everything we learned to this one singular residential/hospitality development of ours. In particular, we made it a priority to use the open courtyards to create a chain of compelling, accessible communal spaces, leading to a public green promenade, all toward our goal of encouraging connection and discovery.

What we learned with Denizen and other such projects is that these full city blocks carry huge untapped potential for revitalizing the public realm and the whole experience of urban living. But these exciting possibilities are still far from being realized, and that's because most city blocks remain bifurcated into many different siloed pieces.

Clearly, it's easier when one controls the whole block, like we did with Denizen. When that's not the case, even if you do everything right and build in relation to what's already there, like we did with Parcel 8, you have no idea what's going to happen down the road. Years later, the neighboring buildings could be demolished, and new structures might go up that completely change the dynamic of the block and the interplay between its architectural components.

That's why we're trying to spread the word and start a conversation among our peers around the idea of dialogue between buildings. Even if we can't control what comes after, the hope is that new generations of architects will embrace the same envelope-expanding mentality.

If this strikes readers as a wildly utopian vision, keep in mind that nothing happens overnight. It's not that we're naïve to the realities of the business but rather that, as with many of the concepts we put forth in this book, we consider our holistic approach a true win-win, a good thing for everyone involved, serving the interest of all parties, from the developer and building owner to the tenants and greater community.

Moreover, there are ways to impact an entire city block and create something extraordinary even when you don't control it yourself. For example, we've proposed a new city regulation in New York to encourage developers to bestow some of their private land to the public in exchange for increased height limits on their buildings, which would in itself help bring the kind of diverse typologies and mixed uses we espouse to our city blocks.

In illustrating to the powers that be how this would all work, we used a theoretical example of Manhattan's Flower District and how it could potentially be transformed. Located at the crossroads of various iconic city landmarks and public parks where community and commerce once flourished, this historic neighborhood has struggled mightily for decades now. It was a very different era back when hundreds of flower vendors filled these midtown blocks; as traffic and cars began to overpower pedestrians, it became harder and harder to maintain the social and economic fabric that once existed.

Now, to bring human density back to this area, we have to look once again at the vital role of city-block courtyards. In Manhattan, these courtyards make up a staggering 40 percent of all open outdoor space in the borough. But they're often hidden and neglected. By granting new air rights to buildings in exchange for opening the courtyards to the public, over time we believe this new arrangement could have the effect of reactivating the Flower District and injecting more life and excitement at the street level.

We are excited about our proposal for all sorts of reasons having to do with environment, social, and economic sustainability. But we bring it up here to show how even when you don't control the whole city block, you can still apply the same thinking and fundamental concepts, even using the existing infrastructure of these urban courtyards, to expand the envelope.

LOCATION 123 Melrose Street, Brooklyn, NY
CLIENT All Year Management
SIZE 1,000,000 SF
TEAM Eran Chen, Ryoko Okada, Chris Berino, Francois Blehaut, Katherine Mendez, Yaarit Sharoni, June Kim, Yuval Borochov, Carolina Moscoso, Vi Nguyen, Heidi Theunissen, Joshua Wujek, Kristina Kesler, Brona Waldron, Seung Bum Ma, Brian Lee, Adrienne Milner, Roman Falcon, Sojin Park, Steven Kocher, Paul Kim, Alex Sarria, Chia-Min Wang, Ascuncion Tapia, Tulika Lokapur, Jaehong Chung, Dawoon Jung, Joohwan Seo, Charles Burke, Emma Pfeiffer, Jennifer Endozo, Hadas Brayer, Shraddha Balasubramaniam, Gokce Saygin Batista

DENIZEN

About 40 percent of the open space in Manhattan is captured inside city-block courtyards, yet this outdoor space is underutilized, unpopulated, and often used only as storage space. Even in the best of cases, courtyards serve as private gardens or are highly fragmented between private parcels, subdivided with fences, temporary structures, and inconsistent landscape.

As underused and ignored resources, the roofs of New York act very similarly to the city's courtyards. And while differences in height may make it hard to envision an interlaced structural fabric, similar incentives could be given to buildings, co-ops, and condo boards to negotiate these disparities and create large-scale rooftop gardens.

In Bushwick, Denizen encompasses a full city block with one million square feet of apartment units. This scale offered us an unprecedented opportunity to explore this idea. We started by looking very closely at the typology of a New York City block and how to apply it to a singular building. In a project of this magnitude, it would have been inconceivable for us to neglect open courtyards and roofs. We made it a point to occupy both territories with communal spaces and build new typologies by which these resources could be used as parks, meeting grounds, and amenity sites.

Our approach yielded 17,850 square feet of public park, which bisects the development with a green promenade. The two building masses are further perforated by a sequence of meandering, interconnected courtyards which ultimately lead to the promenade. Within the courtyard areas, lushly landscaped and partially covered walkways and corridors give way to a parade of plazas, and accessible amenities designed to continue to promote a sense of community in this increasingly vibrant area.

Complementing the structure and efficiency of a more typical grid, the layout encourages both leisure and discovery, the guiding principles of the design. To support the vibrant local art scene, ODA collaborated with local artists to commission all of the art in the complex.

The landscaping at Denizen became a way of unifying the neighborhood and at the same time offering tenants a safe and secluded park of their own, with 60,000 square feet of private rooftop garden at their disposal with the best views of Manhattan.

Illuminated murals in Denizen's single-loaded corridors act as way-finding for residents as well as displays of public art for the community at large. Mural by Mantra for the Bushwick Collective.

The placement of Denizen's many
interconnected courtyards creates
60,000 square feet of landscaped
rooftop space.

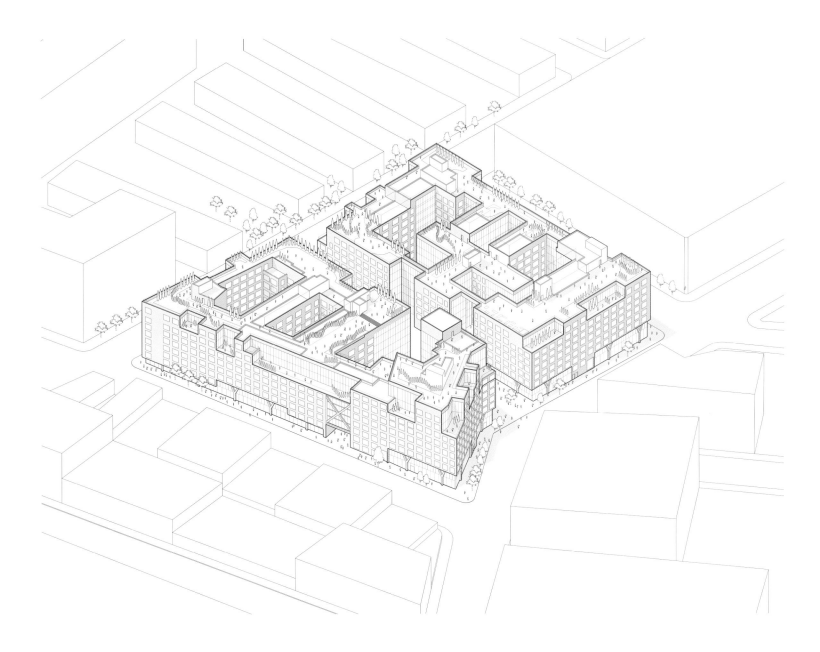

FACING PAGE TOP: The two-building complex is divided by a public park aimed at providing a safe, landscaped destination for the neighborhood to gather.

FACING PAGE BOTTOM: The facade uses oversized bricks to break down the massive scale of the building.

FOLLOWING SPREAD: The interior courtyards offer a secondary pedestrian experience and become the social heart of the building.

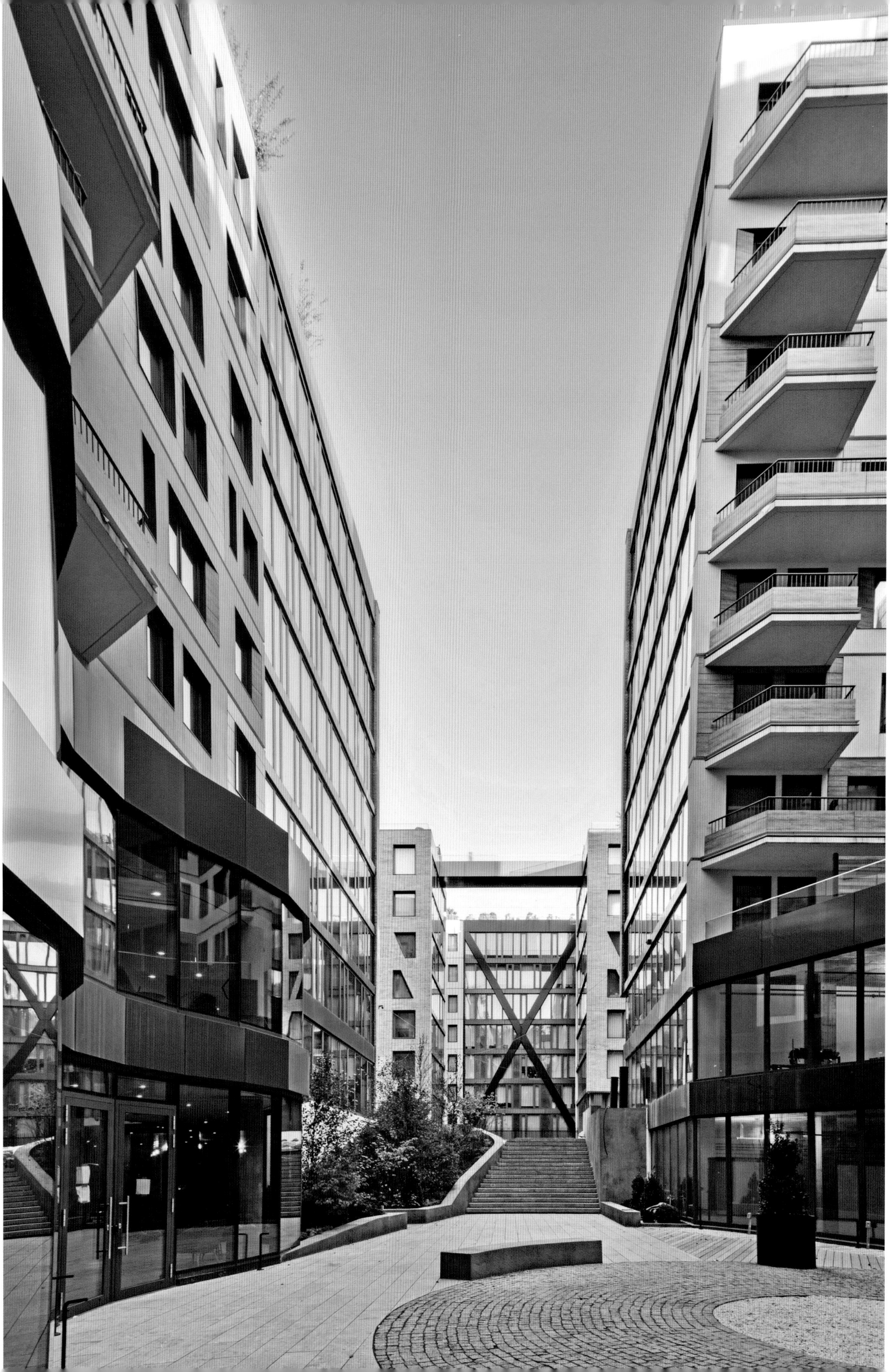

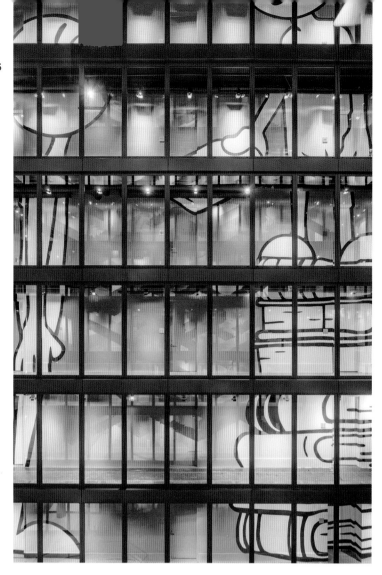

ABOVE: Commissioned public art, such as this mural by Eric Inkala, connects the building to its artistic neighborhood.

FACING PAGE: The building includes murals by (clockwise from top left) Kai, Spiros Naberezny, Aaron Li-Hill, and Eric Inkala.

FOLLOWING SPREAD: Large-scale work, by artists Spiros Naberezny and Chris Soria line the hallways, while the bowling alley features work by Aaron Li-Hill, and the pool features a work by Pixel Pancho.

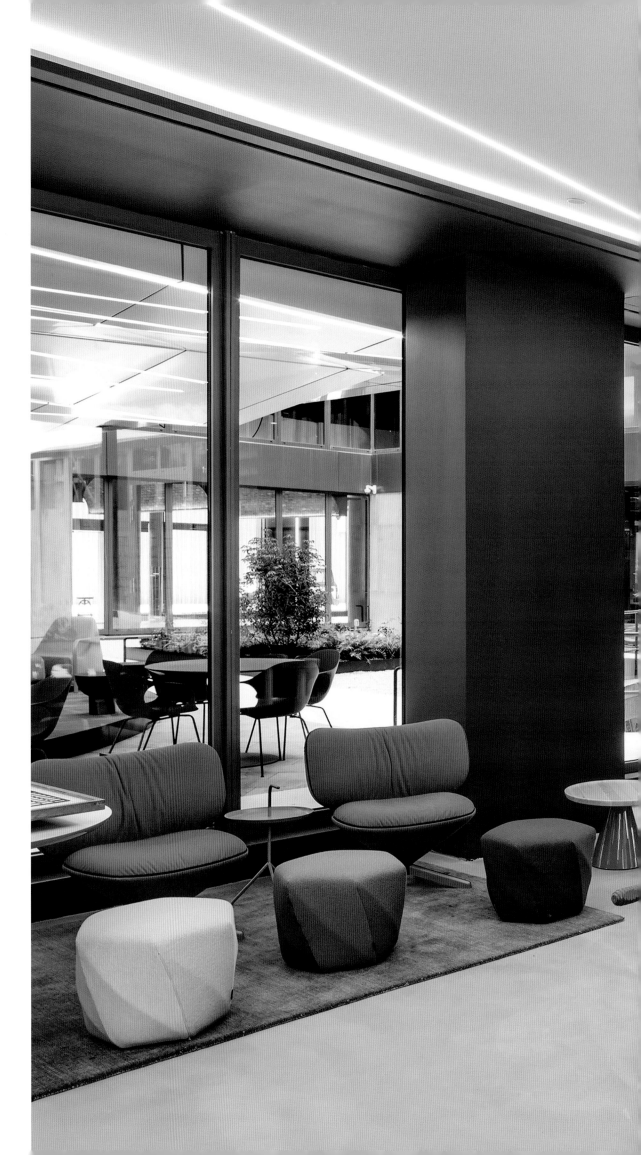

Ground floor amenity spaces emphasize natural light and air with floor-to-ceiling windows that connect residents to the outdoors.

Interior materials reflect the industrial history of this part of the city, including the co-working lounge, which is clad in reclaimed oak, pine, and Douglas fir wood.

FOLLOWING SPREAD: Rooftop amenities serve both practical and entertainment purposes, from the fully operational hydroponic urban farm to the mini golf course.

LOCATION	10 Montieth Street, Brooklyn, NY
CLIENT	The Rabsky Group
SIZE	350,000 SF
TEAM	Eran Chen, P. Christian Bailey, Francois Blehaut, Jason Bourgeois, Karen Evans, Francesco Asaro, Audrey Topp, Kristina Kesler, Brian Lee, Seung Bum Ma, Yongchun Choi, Heidi Theunissen, Nathan Tunkelrot, Hadas Brayer, Sudarshan Venkatraman, Brona Waldron, Yoonah Choi

THE RHEINGOLD

Encapsulating one full block in Bushwick, on the site of the once-famed Rheingold Brewery, this project's distinct modular form creates a pixelated facade with cascading terraces for apartments at affordable and market rates. The streetscape is brought up to the exterior and creates an inhabited facade on all four sides of the block. The building invites residents into an environment of accessibility and connectivity, one that celebrates user experience and champions shared perspective.

The seven-story, mixed-use building contains inner and outer courtyards, and an expansive green rooftop. The sloping angles create a more organic terrain with longer sun exposure for the courtyards and allow for direct horizontal connections from the upper four floors. In this way, living space extends beyond each apartment's four walls with ample outdoor space. Making full use of this often-neglected available space, the design was created with the goal of providing residents many of the urban elements that the area is currently lacking.

Nestled in the center is an interior courtyard that serves as a visual and physical connector, providing additional outdoor recreational space. On the roof, a 100-foot truss bridges between the open courtyard, creating a view deck within views to Manhattan.

Apartments blend with their surrounding outdoor space, designed as an extension of each home. Outside of each unit, residents have access to more than 40 shared amenities, professional workspaces, 70,000 square feet of communal outdoor space, and murals by local artists (in partnership with the Bushwick Collective).

The interior courtyard is a quiet oasis in the city.

A dynamic facade activates the
busy corner.

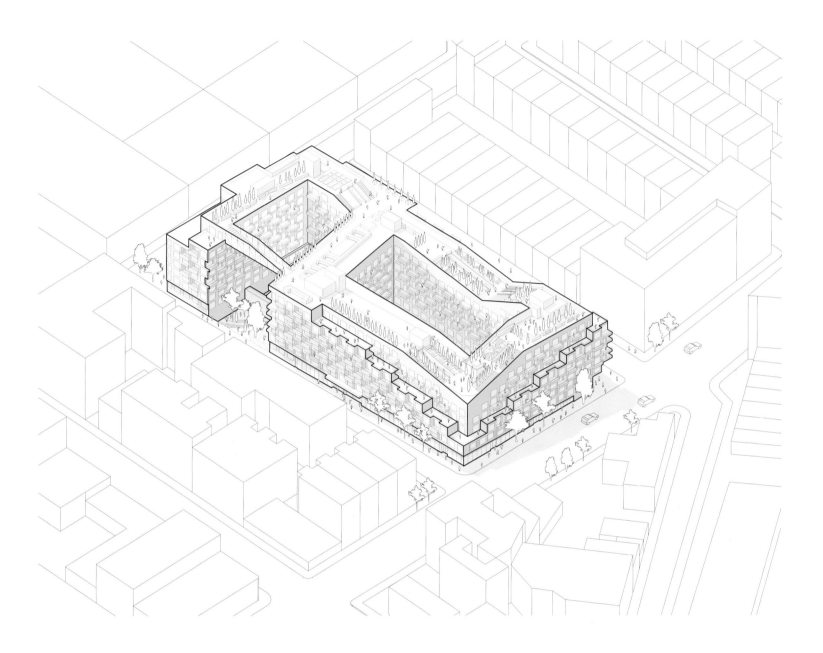

FACING PAGE TOP: Residential
balconies overlook the communal
courtyard garden and encourage visual
connection between neighbors.

FACING PAGE BOTTOM: A custom
designed bridge connects two parts
of the rooftop over the courtyard.

Color animates the facades both
on the street side and to the interior
of the building.

Amenity spaces occur on various levels
of the building, including on the roof.

LOCATION	420 Kent Avenue, Brooklyn, NY
CLIENT	Spitzer Enterprises
SIZE	800,000 SF
TEAM	Eran Chen, Olivera Grk, Ryoko Okada, P. Christian Bailey, Kris Levine, Francois Blehaut, Sunggu Lee, Bernhard Stocker, Dongyoung Kim, Soo Bum You, Zachary Zeller, Jean-Baptiste Berteloot, Woody Wu, Carolina Moscoso, Charmee Donga, Christopher Payan, So Jin Park, Piotr Lewicki, Brona Waldron, Roman Falcon, Shraddha Balasubramaniam, Elizabeth Snow, June Kim, Ninoshka Rachel Henriques, Mingchao Wan, Caroline Remignon, Chia-Min Wang, Matthew Wasnewsky, Sudarshan Venkatraman, Steven Kocher, Sejung Kim, Emma Pfeiffer, Jaehong Chung, UnJae Pyon

420 KENT

The vast majority of rectangularly extruded towers in New York City are the formal result of many historic, contextual, and practical influences. For years, the archetypal curtain wall towers were the dedicated homes of massive corporations, and as the city's population density increased, our habitats naturally adopted a similar two-dimensional shape. The big box concept created an inherent hierarchy, where four corners were most desirable—shaping the corner apartment, corner office, and corner view—while leaving the remaining spaces forgotten and unprioritized. In 420 Kent, we challenge this hierarchy by designing a tower where most dwelling units are a corner apartment.

By using two standard floor plans and mirroring them around the central axis, we created three distinct 22-floor towers featuring multidimensional facades while 80 percent of the total count of apartments are in a corner condition. Adding this third dimension to the envelope provides a platform for intimate moments of interaction, both indoors and out.

Units visually connect to the city, with northern sightlines onto the Williamsburg Bridge, the East River, and eastern vistas of downtown Manhattan. The buildings are simultaneously rooted in their neighborhood. 420 Kent's promenade adds to the communal boardwalk stretching from Greenpoint all the way to Dumbo.

The glass towers blend in with the city and the sky, becoming a backdrop for life around it.

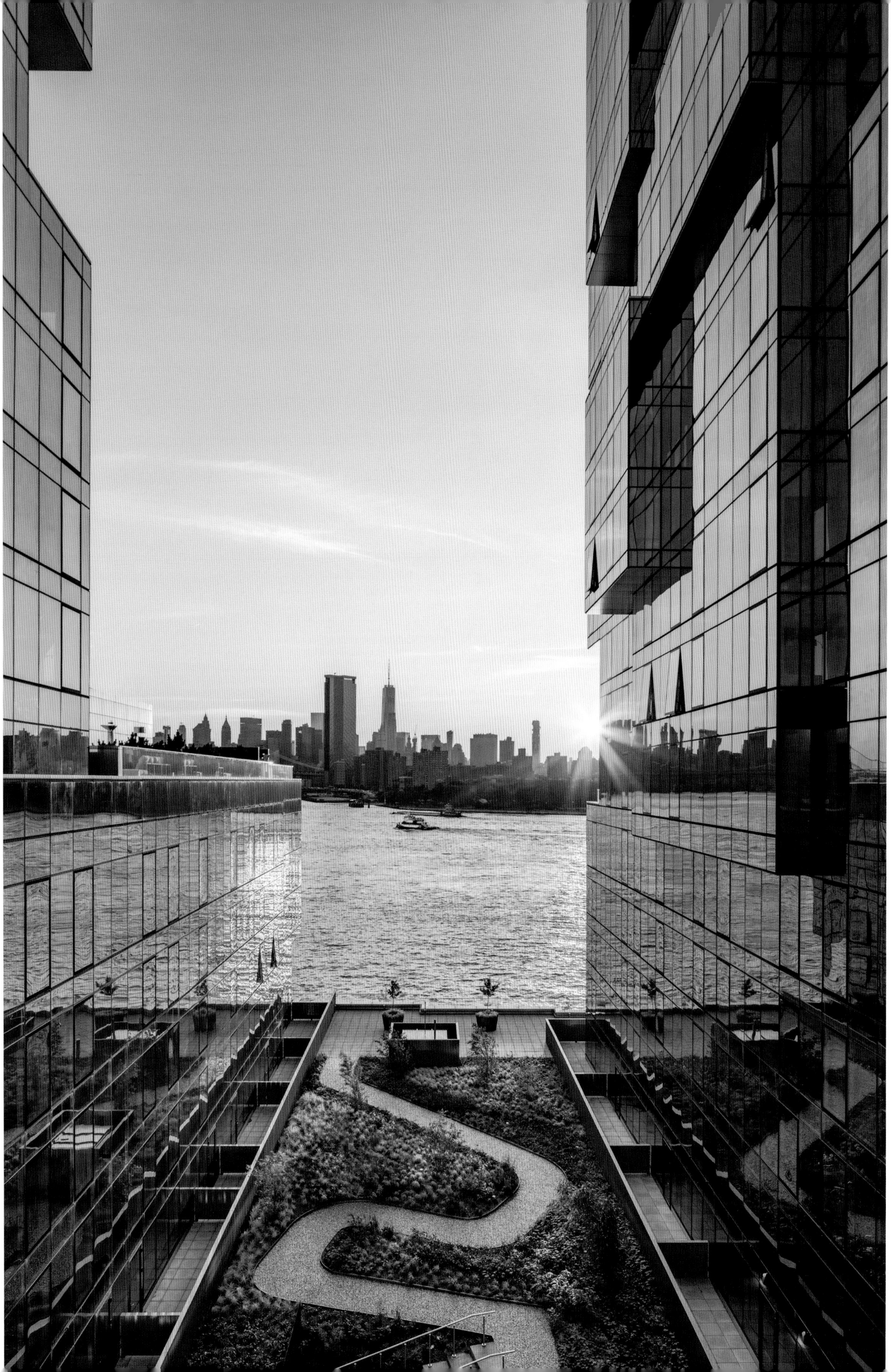

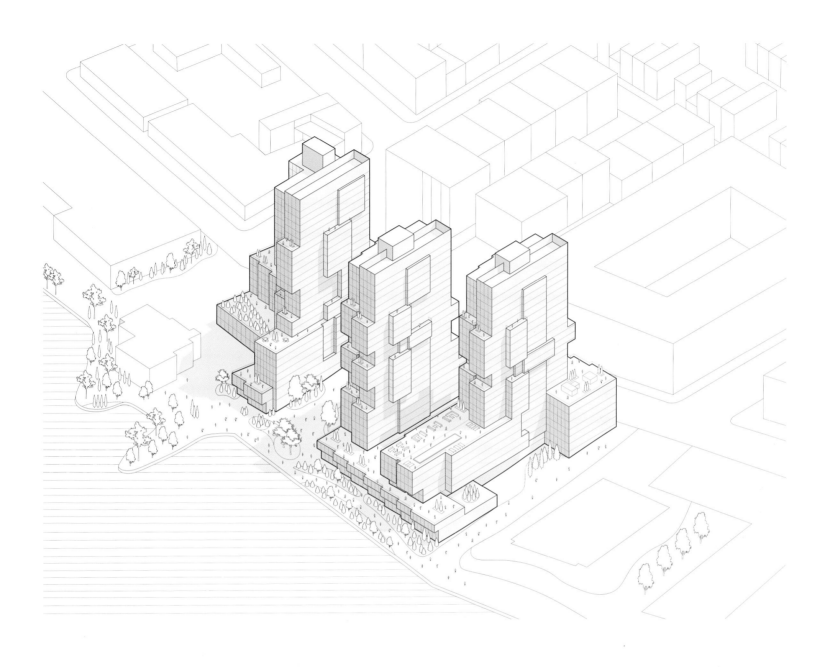

FACING PAGE: Voids between the
buildings are enhanced with lush
gardens.

FOLLOWING SPREAD: The interior
material palette highlights rich
natural materials, such as reclaimed
wood and Corten steel.

Interior spaces enjoy expansive views
across the river.

A light color palette dissolves the boundary between inside and out, creating a welcoming gathering space for residents and guests.

The facade becomes a seamless
extension of the water and the sky.

LOCATION	Southwest Waterfront, Washington, D.C.
CLIENT	PN Hoffman
SIZE	385,000 SF
TEAM	Eran Chen, P. Christian Bailey, Ryoko Okada, Vi Nguyen, June Kim, Alex Tehranian, Michael Unsicker, Matt Adler, Natsumi Oba, Brian Lee, Audrey Topp, Seung Bum Ma, Karen Feilgut, Dawoon Jung, Joohwan Seo, Shixiao Zhang, Jaehong Chung, Joshua Wujek, Shraddha Balasubramaniam

PARCEL 8 AT THE WHARF

Once home to the Municipal Fish Market, this southwest quadrant riverfront area in Washington, D.C., is now a vibrant mixed-use neighborhood. As part of this urban transformation, Parcel 8 is a single, united structure featuring two distinct buildings—residential and hospitality. As can be found in many of our projects, the building's facade is not presented as a two-dimensional plane, but a complex three-dimensional extension, strengthening inside-outside connections and increasing visual interplay between different parts of the building.

One side of the structure climbs to form residences while the other side recedes to establish a hotel, creating clear visual distinction. The building activates the site by connecting to the Potomac River and the surrounding urban context.

In this building, we investigated the traditional U-shaped mass of three bars with a courtyard oriented toward the waterfront. Considering the prime waterfront location, mass was removed from the east bar to create a series of terraces, ascending the height of the building. The building area subtracted from the east bar is added to the west bar as a cantilever, optimizing waterfront views.

The resulting building considers that its two programs have different view requirements. While the hotel wants to offer views for a short period of time, the residential wing wants to preserve a sense of privacy from the constantly changing hotel guests nearby. By stepping back and forward, each wing clears its views, and the residents are offered terraces.

Walking down the Wharf waterfront, the transparent base welcomes street life into its restaurants and shops, activating the main pedestrian path. The building's massing results in visually draping greenery coupled with a courtyard design visible from the street level that visually overlaps with the nearby public park, bringing a sense of unity between the building uses and the surrounding context.

Parcel 8's pool deck is shared between residents and hotel guests, creating an ever-changing community for social interaction.

The building offers both residences and a hotel, each distinctly articulated in its massing and facade.

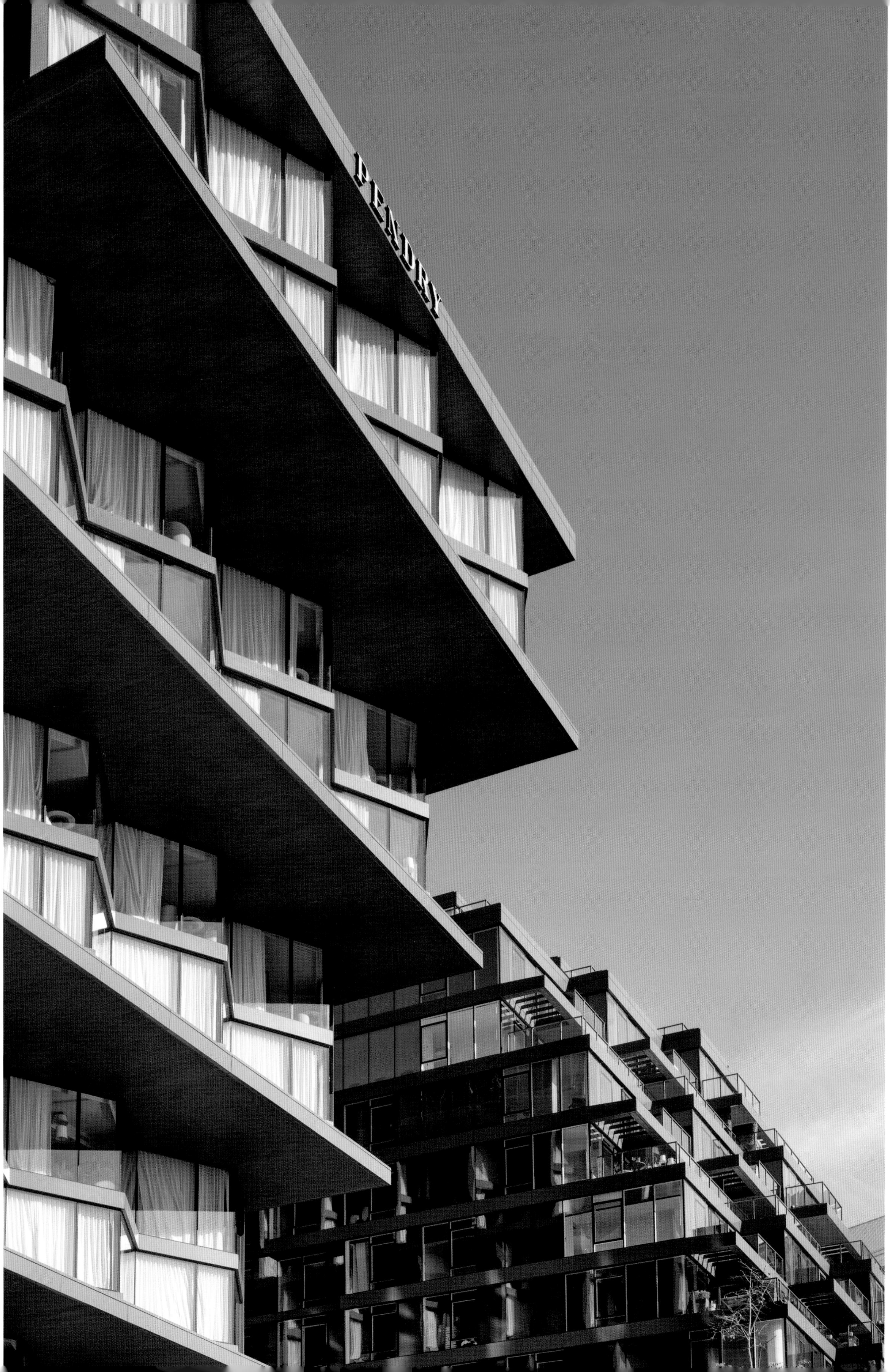
PENDRY

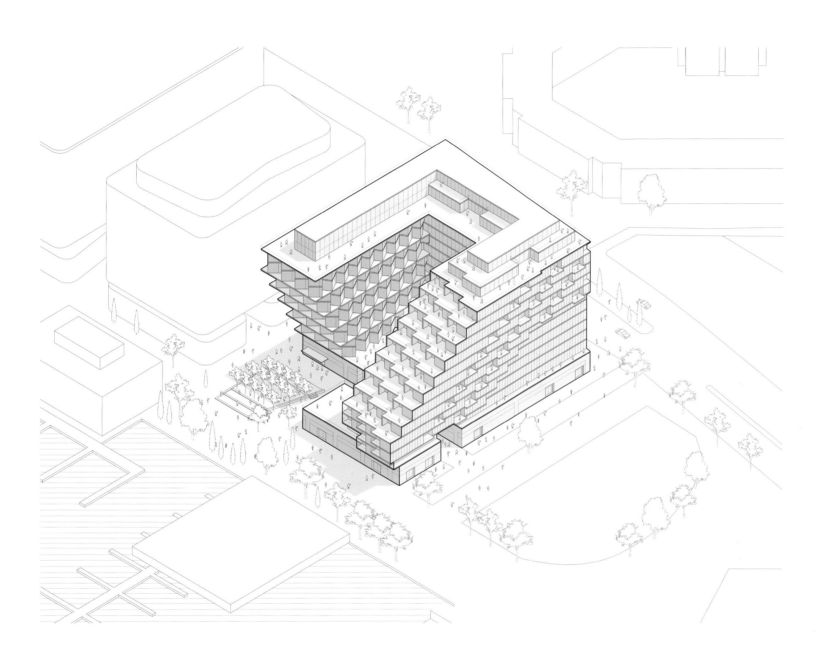

While part of the same building,
the residences and hotel maintain
their privacy.

LOCATION	1201 Half Street SE, Washington, D.C.
CLIENT	JBG
SIZE	456,000 SF
TEAM	Eran Chen, Ryoko Okada, P. Christian Bailey, Katherine Mendez, Jason Bourgeois, Karen Evans, Joshua Wujek, Brian Lee, Come Menage, Vi Nguyen, Emma Pfeiffer, Chia-Min Wang, Hayden Shin

WEST HALF

Steps from Nationals Park in the redeveloped riverfront Navy Yard neighborhood of Washington, D.C., stands West Half—an 11-story mixed-use development, which links residents to the surrounding community in a uniquely contextual and site-specific way. The project serves not just as a visual complement to the neighboring cultural landmark, but also prioritizes the experience of the building "from the inside-out."

The residential floors are filled with apartment layouts that break the typical Washington, D.C., building mass into a more human scale that connects indoor and outdoor, and increases the amount of light and air. Discarding a more traditional form, the building's shape gradually cants as it ascends, echoing the existing gradient of Nationals Park and fostering a graceful transition between the street, structure, and stadium. This subtle shift provides all units with seven feet of outdoor terrace space and offers nearly half of the apartments direct sightlines onto the field of the stadium.

The increasingly vibrant pedestrian life on this major entry point to the stadium—bolstered by West Half's two floors of retail space—blurs the threshold between inside and outside, public and private, allowing people to participate with the world beyond their doors in a continuous cascade of activity. The building features a rooftop pool and a landscaped courtyard nestled below cantilevered balconies that line the interior of the building's U-shaped footprint.

The building blurs the boundary between inside and outside, with interstitial spaces that offer a moment of calm in this vibrant part of the city.

The gradual setback of the building offers a transition from the street and establishes a relationship to the monumental scale of the adjacent stadium.

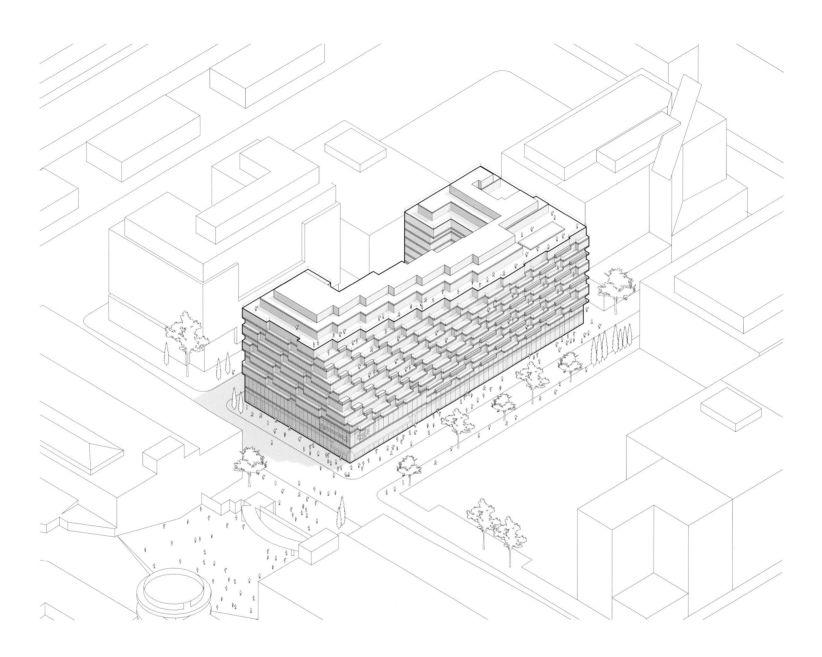

FACING PAGE: The muted palette of the
interiors shapes a calming oasis on this
continually active site.

An inside-out design connects interior spaces to the surrounding neighborhood.

FOLLOWING SPREAD: The building's gradual setbacks offer all residences a terrace.

LOCATION	1265 Washington Boulevard, Detroit, MI
CLIENT	Bedrock Detroit
SIZE	486,760 SF
TEAM	Eran Chen, Ryoko Okada, Gene Pyo, Francois Blehaut, Chris Berino, Akshay Surana, Chris Krambias, Alex Ward, Gregory Kamback, Jessica Schoen, Prachi Bhinde, Celia Julve, Tulika Lokapur, Adrienne Milner, Matt Hallstein, Kevin Hall, Jaehong Chung, Diana Tao, Khue Truong, Chia-Min Wang, Jason Bourgeois, Karen Evans, Tamara Jamil

BOOK TOWER

An adaptive reuse project in the heart of Downtown Detroit, the renovated Book Tower offers a mix of residential, hospitality, retail, and office space, following more than a decade of vacancy. The conversion of this legacy structure balances reverence for the remarkable history of the Book Tower, and the vision and ambition to deliver a civic hub that complements the movement happening in Downtown Detroit.

The 486,760 square-foot structure, which was designed by Louis Kemper in 1926 in an Italian Renaissance style, was originally built as an office tower and took a decade to complete. An extensive exterior restoration was recently completed, including the replacement of over 2,000 historically accurate windows and a full restoration of the ornamental cornice complete with caryatid statues.

The Book Tower has been an iconic part of Detroit's skyline for nearly a century, and the new design preserves the historic details that has made this building a landmark in the city. Expanding on the tower's programming and existing structures, the design creates nearly 500,000 square feet of mixed-use space. The building's residents and public share amenity spaces throughout the different levels as well as entertaining spaces on the roof of the Book Building portion of the property.

The Book Tower serves as a connector, an attractor in Detroit's Historic District. The plans include a blend of public and private space, including a variety of public amenities in the form of retail, galleries, restaurants, and cafés that anchor the base of the building and activate the sidewalks. The design recuperates the original qualities of the public floors, especially the Glazed Atrium in the heart of the building, which was tarnished by decades of soot and nicotine. With only a few historical photos and a hand drawn sketch, we were able to reimagine the original structure. Our team recognized 12 patterns in the glass and crystal, reconstructed them in Rhino, and tweaked the geometry to fit the current dimensions of the space. The renovation of the historic glass skylight underlines the civic value of this public hall in the landscape of great atriums in Detroit.

With open sight lines to Washington Boulevard and Grand River Avenue, the public spaces add to the city's pedestrian experience, while the alleyway is enlivened with landscape and seating areas as an extension of the interior public space. Accessible from multiple sides, the building will serve as a point of engagement in the city center.

A careful renovation of the interior and exterior of Book Tower celebrates this icon in the center of Detroit.

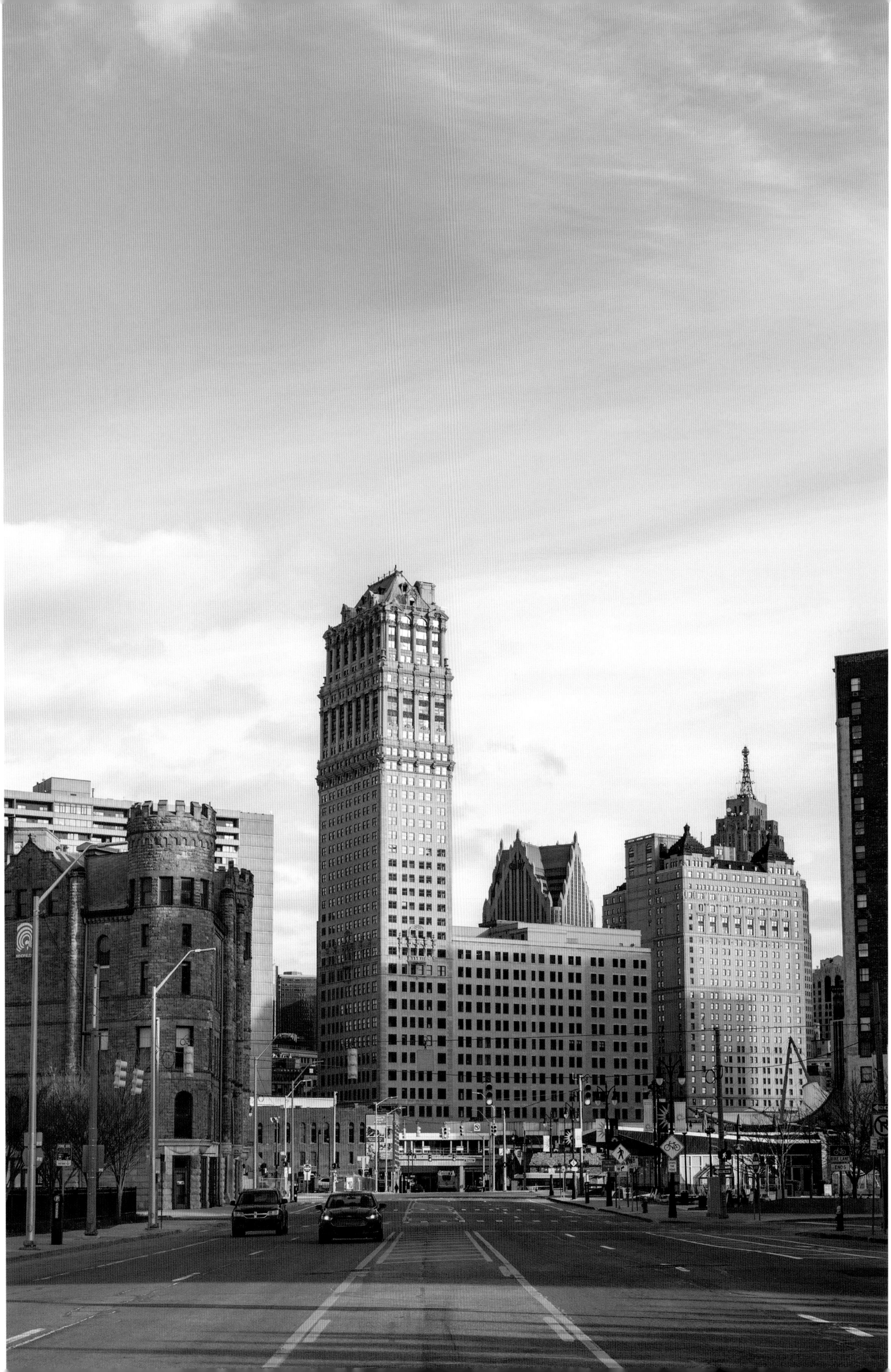

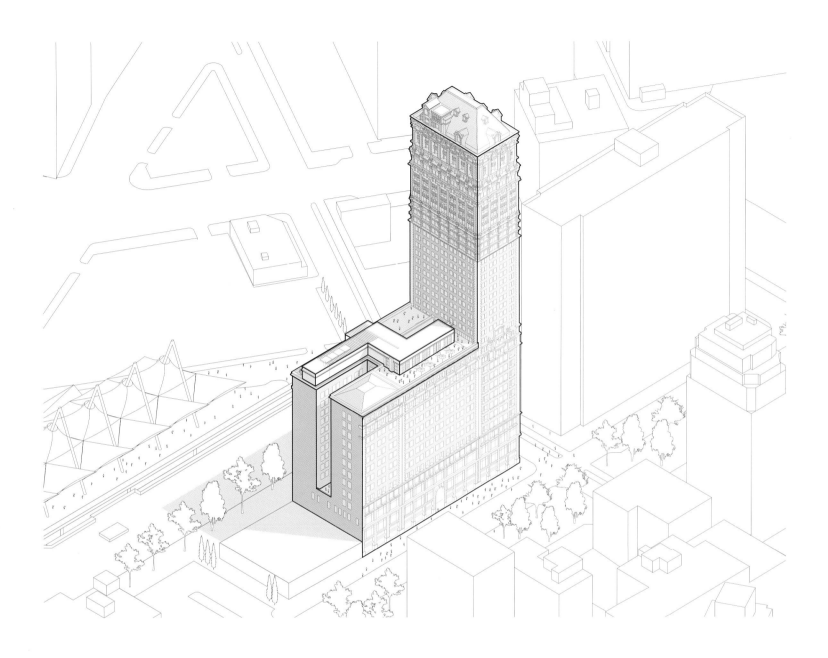

FACING PAGE: Book Tower is a visual landmark in downtown Detroit. New ground level public spaces connect the building to the city.

FOLLOWING SPREAD: The careful renovation of the historic glass skylight brings new life to this civic space.

NEIGH
HOOD

Over the course of this book so far, we've looked at expanding the architectural envelope at the scale of the individual apartment unit, the building, and the whole block, all toward better meeting the changing needs of city dwellers and the changing face of our streetscapes and urban environments. But when it comes to positively impacting entire neighborhoods, our endeavor takes on a greater urgency. That's because, in places like New York, Washington, D.C., and San Francisco, and other big cities around the world, from Santiago to Rotterdam, not only are there massive housing crises, but in central business districts, huge office buildings sit largely empty, foot traffic has evaporated, and the surrounding restaurants and retail establishments are on life support.

Part of the challenge is that these entire neighborhoods were built predominantly for office use, and the commercial buildings in these districts have been losing their appeal for some time now because they're just not suited to today's needs. This problem existed before, but when the pandemic hit, it was a near fatal blow—especially for certain areas where the office buildings are outdated.

We're seeing this same issue in so many of our major metropolises. It all adds up to a multilayered urban problem that not only makes these particular neighborhoods unsafe, inert, and unattractive, but also negatively affects the livelihood of millions, including all those who work in the shops and restaurants on the street level.

It can all start to feel like we're stuck. So how did we get here, and what can be done?

Any answer to this question must involve expansion of the public realm. We must look at neighborhoods with fresh eyes— and this means flipping the usual formulation about "served" and "serviced" spaces. In the past, the public realm at the ground floor was in service of the daytime office population. And the human density created by the white-collar commuters served to infuse livelihood at the street level.

But now that all needs to flip. The steady stream of office workers is gone and very few street activators remain. We need to build an active public realm on the ground that doesn't rely solely on commercial tenants. Instead, it will draw crowds of people from all around the city—and serve *them*.

Ultimately, it will also help fill the buildings above. All the excitement on the ground will increase the market value and general appeal of the real estate on top, not just for office use but every aspect of our lives. Successful ground floor programs need to include both indoor and outdoor space, more green space, and more public areas in general. Moreover, what we design at the ground floor has to be unique and interesting.

We saw the power and potential of revitalized streetscapes— and particularly our concept of "inclusionary retail"—with our Innovation QNS project in Astoria. There, we had the opportunity to design a whole chunk of a neighborhood from scratch. It's a full five city blocks, and we dedicated a quarter of the private land to create public space. The programming at the ground floor will be catered around the needs of both the residents and the entire surrounding neighborhood. We landscaped and hardscaped it all beautifully and made sure there were ample bike lanes and pedestrian passageways.

Our urban renewal efforts are all geared toward creating a real destination, an attractive neighborhood that people would want to live in. And like with all the envelope-expanding approaches we've covered in this book, whether we're talking about a neighborhood, a block, a building, or an individual apartment, there's an important distinction to be made here between needs and wants, between an old model centered around accommodating our basic functional requirements and new ones based on our deeper human desires.

The current situation we're facing is not the first time in history that cities, and the people who build them, have had to accommodate major transitions, such as mass migrations, population booms, economic shifts, and the like. Change is good. But now we're looking at a world where, as discussed in the introduction, many of our everyday needs are being taken care of digitally. So our solutions for accommodating this historical transition that we're living through need to be concentrated on different typologies for urban life.

Expanding the envelope at every scale is about engagement, connection, and excitement, from the most intimate realm to the most public and everywhere in between. In this chapter, we explore our projects that will come to life in the next few years. These designs, from single towers to entire urban plans, have the potential to reinvigorate their neighborhoods and change the way people experience them. Whether it's the adaptive reuse of an unused parking garage, or an entire city designed from the ground-up, these projects represent what we at ODA believe can improve the lives of people in cities everywhere, and add a little fun.

In redefining quality of life for our current era, our driving impulse must be to foster these principles—engagement, connection, and excitement—across different communities and create a sense of belonging.

Cities have always been the best place for that, and I believe they always will be.

LOCATION	Coolsingel 42, Rotterdam, The Netherlands
CLIENT	OMNAM Investment Group
SIZE	850,000 SF
TEAM	Eran Chen, Michael Unsicker, Ryoko Okada, Yaarit Sharoni, Juan Roque Urrutia, Katherine Mendez, Steven Kocher, Kevin Muni, Matt Adler, Audrey Topp, Saranya Kanagaraj, Natsumi Oba, Zach Zeller, James Moulder, Matthew Rosen, Nofar Ashuri

POST ROTTERDAM

In Rotterdam's center, the historic former Central Postkantoor remains a testament to the inextinguishable spirit of Rotterdam. Built in 1916, the building was one of the only original structures still standing after Rotterdam Blitz, the aerial bombardment that in 1940 leveled nearly all of the city's historic core. Restoring, designing, and engineering the conversion of such valuable heritage requires the utmost reverence for the remarkable history of the building, but also the vision and ambition to deliver a civic hub worthy of its central setting.

We conceived a dynamic mixed-use design, resolving to both preserve and adapt the Postkantoor's original construction. The POST is a civic node distinguished by seamless connectively; it is not only a memory of the historic strength of Rotterdam, but also signal that Rotterdam continues as a vibrant, connected, center of culture, renewal, and quality of life.

A new 150-meter tower rises toward the rear of the Postkantoor structure and straddles the existing open courtyard at the Rodezand wing. The vaulted plinth of the tower will enhance the experience of the courtyard, coupling it with the Great Hall of the Postkantoor.

The POST tower is a reinterpretation of both urban living and the Postkantoor's architectural assets, extending the elegance of the main hall through to the tower. This modern addition to the city center's Coolsingel district is based on a rigorous investigation combined with the expertise gained over two years working with city partners.

The design mirrors the rhythm of five-meter spacing between columns on the Postkantoor's facade in a stone grid that defines the tower. Designed with nonpareil windows, the POST tower shows openings that vary in size and shape to funnel daylight. This variety sets a break from the series of glass-facade towers along the new Rotterdam skyline and celebrates the elegance of the main hall along its profile.

At the street level, the majestic Great Hall—a vaulted, 1916 marvel soaring almost 22.5 meters in height—will undergo a faithful restoration to serve as the project's public heart, fed by existing entrances at Coolsingel and Meent. A new entrance on Rodezand will render the hall accessible from all sides and will connect with the building's back courtyard to form a sweeping passageway. Throughout the hall and courtyard space, a slew of public amenities—in the form retail, galleries, restaurants, and cafés, many with open sight lines to the adjacent streets, Coolsingel and Rodezand—will add to the city's pedestrian experience.

The upper floors of the Postkantoor, formerly dedicated to the telegraph and telephone services of the post office, will be revived with a five-star hotel operated by Kimpton. Accessible from every side, this monument will, once again, serve as a point of engagement in the city center, a link between Rotterdam Centraal train station, all the way to the bustling Markthal, designed by MVRDV.

The new Postkantoor updates the skyline without rupturing it, and the community is offered a renewed take on a building full of memories. As Rotterdam's population densifies and the skyline expands, creating a gathering place that integrates urban living with a balance of mixed uses results in a civic hub worthy of its origins.

The POST tower vertically extends the historic beauty of the Central Postkantoor.

The POST tower rises with a quiet elegance as a marker of the strength of the original Postkantoor in the center of Rotterdam.

The POST tower bridges old and new architectural landmarks.

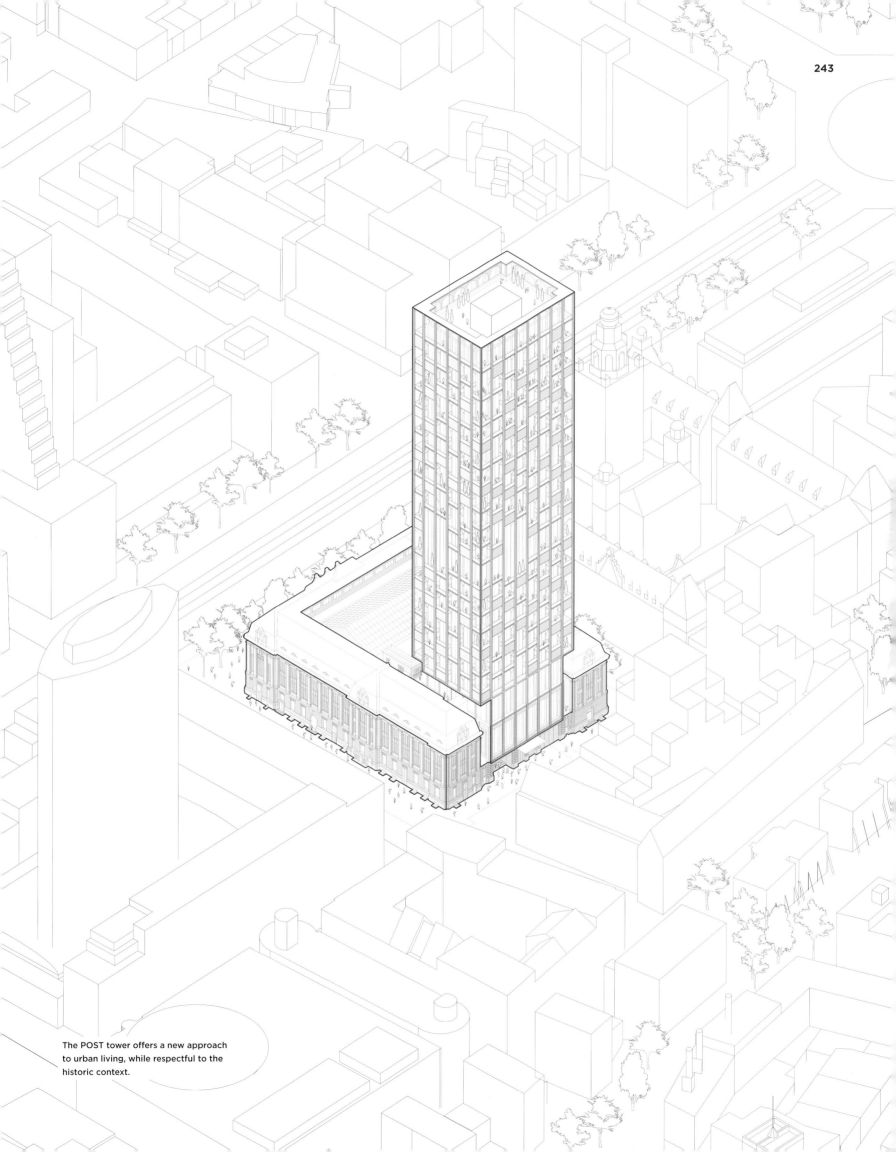

The POST tower offers a new approach to urban living, while respectful to the historic context.

The rhythm of the five-meter spacing between columns is a subtle nod to context that defines the stone grid of the tower.

Inspired by the tactile experience of sending mail, the Kimpton's interior style features bold colors, textures, and finishes reminiscent of ink blots, wax seals, and perforated stamp edges.

The hotel common spaces embrace the hundred-year-old monument's art deco bones.

FOLLOWING SPREAD: At the street level, the majestic Great Hall—a vaulted, 1916 marvel soaring 22.5 meters in height—will undergo a faithful restoration to serve as the project's public heart, fed by existing entrances on two streets. A new entrance on another will render the hall accessible from all sides, and will connect with the building's back courtyard to form a sweeping passageway.

LOCATION	Moscow, Russia
CLIENT	Glavstroy
SIZE	3,000,000 SF
TEAM	Eran Chen, Olivera Grk, Francois Blehaut, Juan Roque Urrutia, Vladimir Chervoniuk, Brian Lee, Yinxing Xu, Michelle Le, Christopher Sjoberg, Diana Tao, Steven Kocher, Jacob Hedaya, Jean-Baptiste Berteloot, Pablo Zepeda, Saranya Kanagaraj, Adrienne Milner, Jaehong Chung, Dan Hoch, Ilya Chistiakov

MAZD

The MAZD master plan for a mixed-use development intends to regenerate industrial zones just outside Moscow City. The city has a significant number of these post-industrial sites in valuable areas, directly aligned with main transportation vectors.

The MAZD area is 9.3 hectares and will, in many ways, affect the further development of the surrounding neighborhood. The master plan is created as a meaningful contribution to the development of this urban fabric—one that will, overtime, set the guidelines for a more pedestrian, green, and mixed redevelopment, and one that will become a destination in this valuable part of the city.

The MAZD Territory will be an innovative neighborhood, establishing a visible marker along the Third Ring Road of Moscow's multipurpose, green, and accessible urban agenda. The new MAZD will update the deployment of public programs along the West sector of the Third Ring Road, close enough to the bustling influence of Moscow City. The proposed schemes follow Moscow's trends for a dense, mixed, and walkable region where architecture and landscape are designed in conjunction. The interweaving of public and recreational spaces with residences and offices strengthens the sense of place that this location much needs.

An iconic roof landmarks MAZD within the city skyline. Below, the residences are strategically organized with courtyards and open sight lines. This brings a human scale to the development and creates two complementing typologies: villas around quiet patios and towers exposed to the far views. In plan the scheme is modular and achieves a close checkerboard balance between open and enclosed spaces. In elevation the scheme is topographical and all uses are arranged under a unifying roof. On the ground, leisure and retail are laid out to enjoy the experience of the continuous park. This modular development can adapt to different typologies, masterplans and can influence the north and south expansions of future developmental stages. The new MAZD will be an iconic and multilevel tapestry of life for leisure and human interaction.

MAZD re-energizes a former industrial zone on the outskirts of Moscow.

The mixed-use development aims to
bring new life to this part of the city.

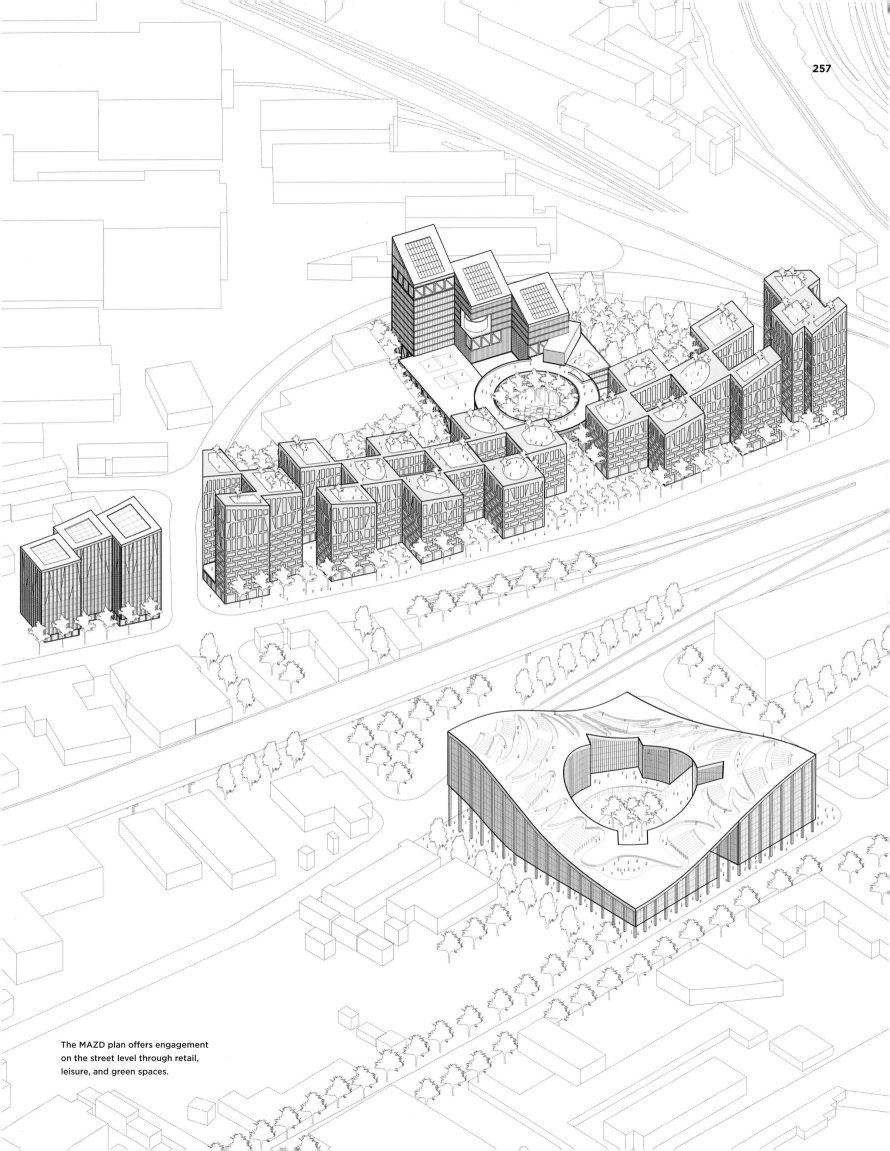

The MAZD plan offers engagement
on the street level through retail,
leisure, and green spaces.

Green spaces run throughout the plan,
adding a grounded sense of place
around which the architecture unfolds.

LOCATION	Astoria, Queens, NY
CLIENT	Silverstein Properties, Kaufman Astoria Studios, and Bedrock Real Estate Partners
SIZE	2,982,000 SF
TEAM	Eran Chen, Michael Unsicker, Olivera Grk, Francois Blehaut, Pablo Zepeda, Dan Hoch, Steven Kocher, Jacob Hedaya, Natsumi Oba, Anirudh Chandar, Amaya D'Souza, Saranya Kanagaraj, Alex Rossetti, Kirat Pandher, Katinka Bosch

INNOVATION QNS

The Innovation QNS master plan aims to bring sustainable economic growth to Astoria, Queens. The design approach embraces the role of the private sector, as well as the valuable feedback and insight from community members and local organizations, to create a diverse, vibrant, walkable, mixed-use district that builds upon Astoria's rich cultural fabric. This master plan opens up two acres of landscaped green space for public use and offers affordable retail and hundreds of affordable apartments.

The plan focuses development on areas with good access to public transportation, activating and revitalizing main thoroughfares, adding open public space, and growing foot traffic to better support existing local businesses. Additional guiding principles are expanding public access to arts, culture, lifetime learning, health and wellness, and other critical services; providing adequate parking; and dedicating space for the tech and creative industries to grow.

In all, the plan includes 3,200 new homes, including 1,440 affordable units. The approved plan also includes dedicated units to serve individuals exiting the shelter system. Innovation QNS also includes thoughtfully programmed and landscaped open space, community health and wellness facilities, a community culture hub, a state-of-the-art multiplex cinema, a new full-service grocery store, and enhanced streetscapes by SWA/Balsley.

The Innovation QNS master plan aims to bring vibrant economic growth to Astoria.

The master plan activates the street level with public spaces and a variety of architectural scales.

Green spaces connect the blocks
and public spaces welcome the
local community.

Increasing foot traffic supports existing local businesses.

LOCATION	Buenos Aires, Argentina
CLIENT	BSD Investments
SIZE	160,000 SF
TEAM	Eran Chen, Michael Unsicker, Francois Blehaut, Matt Boker, Audrey Topp, Michelle Le, Alex Rossetti

PASEO GIGENA

A city can continue to grow horizontally and conquer more territory, and all the infrastructure could be demolished and a new one built to replace it—as has been done for much of history. But as our everyday needs for space evolve alongside rapid technological innovation, existing buildings seem to reach their expiration date earlier and earlier. Instead of demolishing a structure in order to erect a new one, adaptive reuse strategies can help us keep up with the rapid pace of change in our society, giving new life to old structures and hopefully even revitalizing areas of the city in the process.

In Buenos Aires, Paseo Gigena converts a decaying parking structure into a public park and office building, replacing the concrete shell with cafés, restaurants, retail, an open-air promenade, offices, and a sheltered parking lot. Located in between the racecourse and the popular park "El Rosedal de Palermo," Paseo Gigena shapes an iconic new civic space and important point of connectivity for the city, relinking the area that today finds itself divided by this very land plot.

Capitalizing on the unique location on the edge of the active park, the adaptive reuse project completes the park loop by carrying the green path up the side of the building to the landscaped roof and ramping down the other side, connecting back to the park. The rooftop provides a continuation of the public park, complemented by a commercial brewery, as well as private terraces for office tenants, positioning the project as a key juxtaposition of the public and private sectors, unified via nature. The glass facade acts as a mirror to the sky and green surroundings, creating organic curves that erode the edges of the existing parking structure.

Paseo Gigena transforms a former parking structure into a mixed-use complex with a public park on its roof.

The park promenade is accessible from the ground level and gives new pedestrian life to the old car-centric structure.

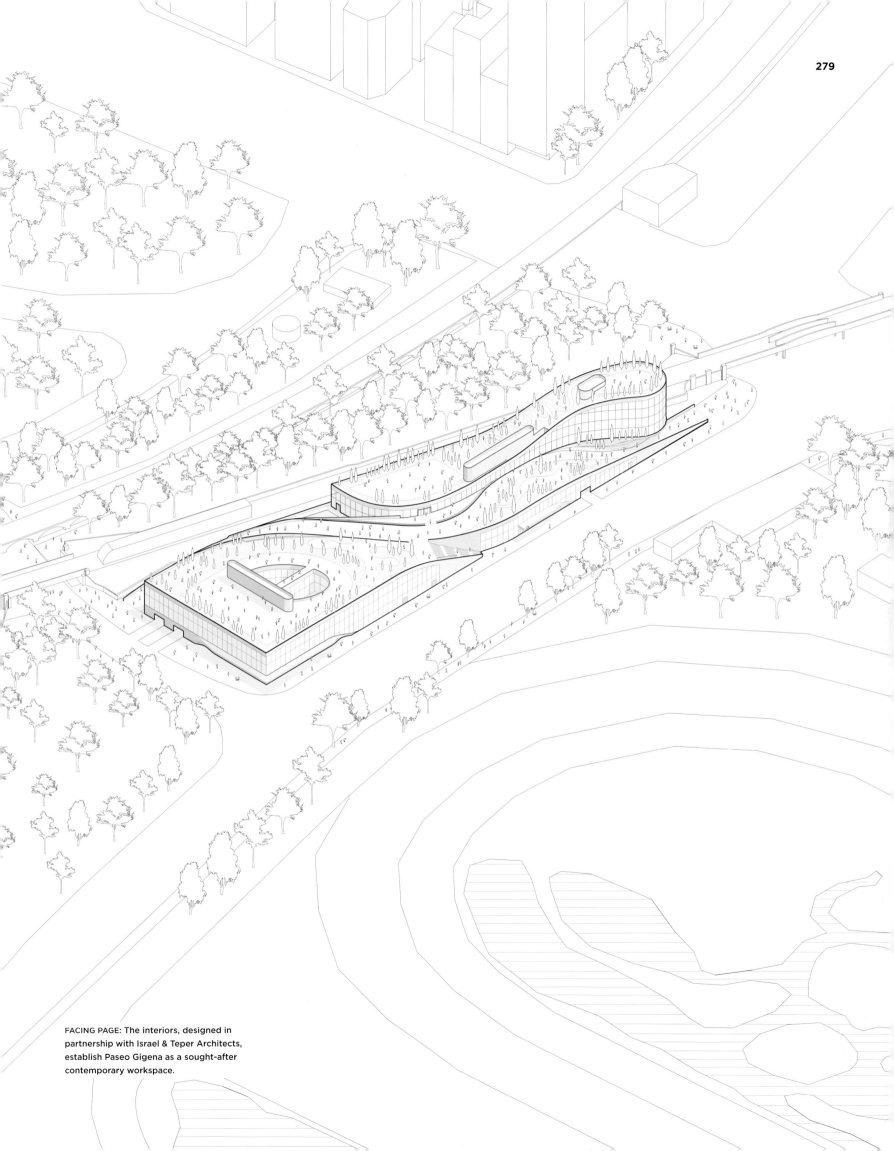

FACING PAGE: The interiors, designed in partnership with Israel & Teper Architects, establish Paseo Gigena as a sought-after contemporary workspace.

LOCATION	Washington, D.C.
CLIENT	Redbrick LMD
SIZE	1,000,000 SF
TEAM	Eran Chen, P. Christian Bailey, Patricia Gortari, Gene Pyo, Keith Sagliocca, Belen Pena, Jamie Niver, Michael Evola, Ryan Barnette, Dan Hoch, Konrad Nieradka, Anirudh Chandar, Lilach Borenstein, Yinxing Xu, Kirat Pandher

BRIDGE DISTRICT

Bridge District Parcel 1 and 2 focus on resiliency and place-making and offer a level of economic, social, and environmental sustainability rarely seen in ground-up development in Washington, D.C. ODA plans to expand the public realm and create pockets of human connectivity and interaction, both indoor and outdoor. The inclusive approach aims to improve the health and wellbeing of the local community and stand as a template for improving life in our cities. The design adds long-term value by meeting environmental goals, future proofing against changing standards, and consumer demands.

The public realm will be enlivened with residents, retail, bike trails, parks, fitness amenities, bars, and restaurants, all meant to create a vibrant and inviting neighborhood just steps from downtown D.C. The entire length of the ground floor along Howard Road, with the exception of the residential lobbies, is devoted to retail, restaurant, and landscaped outdoor areas, activating the street life of the surrounding community.

The buildings meet the ground floor with three residential lobbies and three pocket parks that lead up to a raised amenity courtyard, through a hardscaped sculptural staircase. Connecting the two buildings on the street level is a welcoming porte cochere accessible through a pedestrian plaza, which acts as a drop-off point for cars and bicycles. The ground floor is wrapped in local retail and other food and beverage options. The common landscaped courtyard and green spaces on the second level are activated by the adjacent indoor amenities for the District's residents.

Parcel 1 is a mass-timber residential structure on a concrete podium. Parcel 2 is a post-tension concrete structure encased in a masonry facade. Residents of both buildings will have access to a large program of courtyard and rooftop amenities, from fitness and wellness to co-working and creative spaces meant to offer residents a comfortable work-from-home option. With wraparound balconies and terraces throughout the project, the overall vision for Parcel 1 and 2 is truly an indoor-outdoor experience, connected to the rich nature and river views surrounding it.

Parcels 1 and 2 are separated by a pedestrian plaza and walkway, uninterrupted by car traffic.

While most mass-timber buildings cover the wood with other materials, the Bridge District celebrates the natural material by putting it on display.

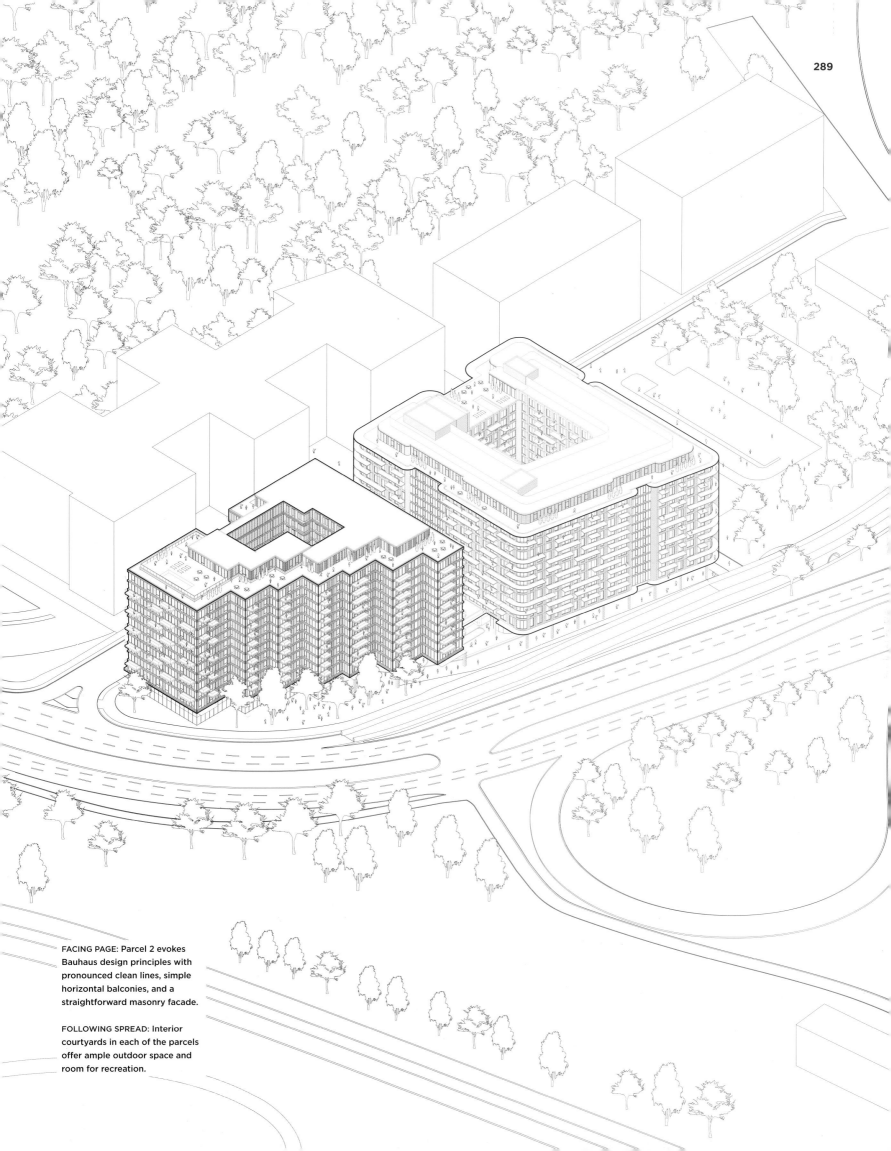

FACING PAGE: Parcel 2 evokes Bauhaus design principles with pronounced clean lines, simple horizontal balconies, and a straightforward masonry facade.

FOLLOWING SPREAD: Interior courtyards in each of the parcels offer ample outdoor space and room for recreation.

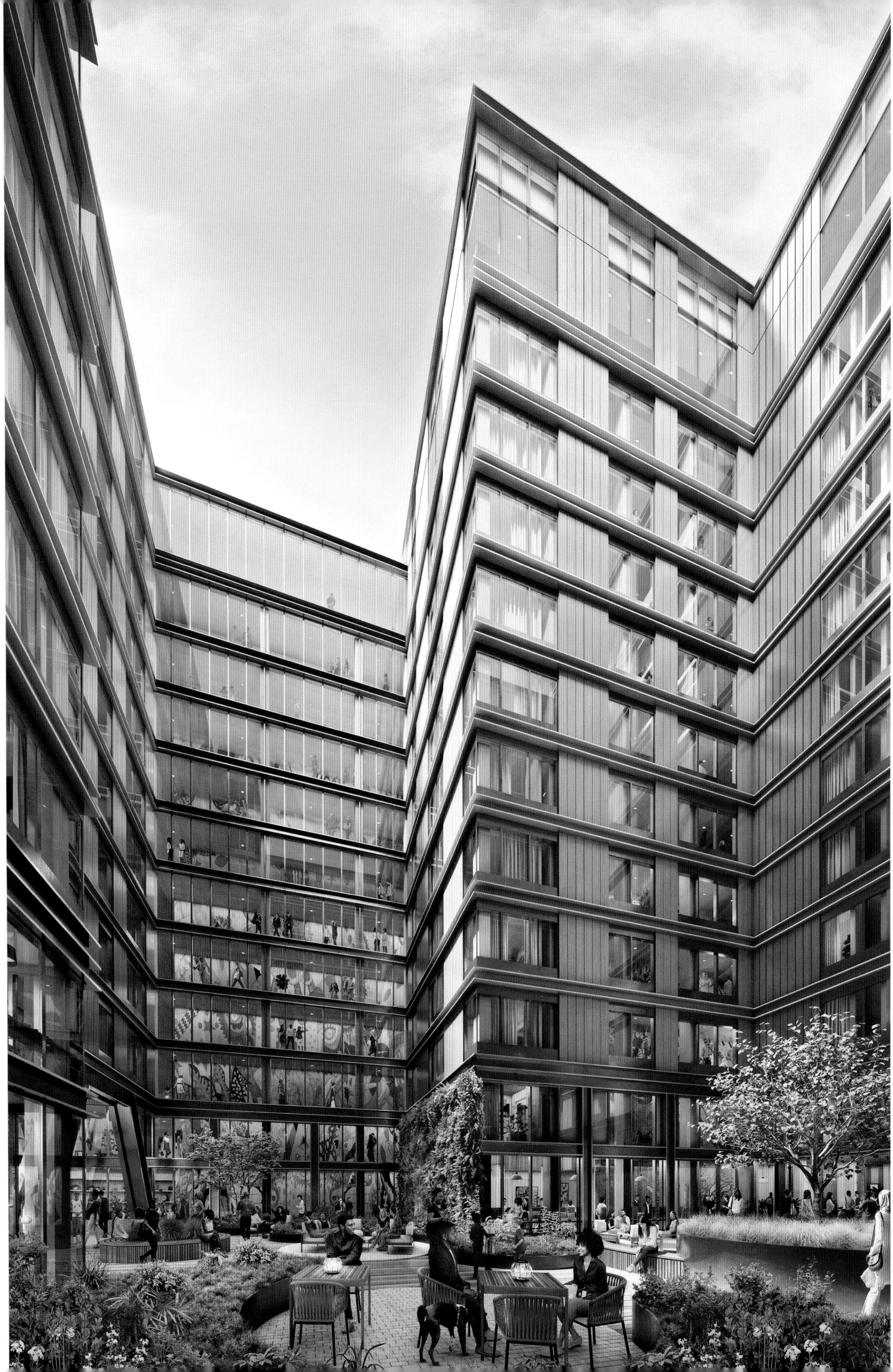

LOCATION 619 Breakers Avenue, Fort Lauderdale, FL
CLIENT Edition Hotels
SIZE 390,000 SF
TEAM Eran Chen, Olivera Grk, Francois Blehaut, Christopher Sjoberg, Michelle Le, Yinxing Xu, Diana Tao, Liwan Zhang

THE NEST

Finding a balance between a strong vertical expression and meaningful street-level engagement can be a challenge, but value can be found in both. In an ocean of hotels, the Nest distinguishes itself not only architecturally but also through its contribution to the vibrancy of its community street life.

The Fort Lauderdale Edition Hotel and Residences situates its tower on the eastern side of the property to take advantage of ocean views and to align with other hotel towers. The lower podium is positioned to the west, where it respects the scale and height of its low-rise residential neighbors.

The building's facade design draws inspiration from the natural tones, flowing lines, and essence of the beloved banyan trees of nearby Bonnet House Garden, the numerous vertical trunks of which create layers of enclosed space within an ever-changing play of sun and shadow. Turning this inspiration on its side, the building's exterior constitutes a medley of natural-toned aluminum bands that envelops and shrouds the various balconies and terraces into a unifying and delicate aesthetic dubbed the Nest.

At the ground floor, the development takes a community-first approach, setting back the building's walls from the street to provide deep, lushly planted landscapes, broad sidewalks, corner plazas, and seating areas across all four of the property's tree-lined frontages. Further enhancing this public realm, multiple retail and food and beverage programs activate these corner plazas, forming social gathering points for the quaint, pedestrian-friendly neighborhood concentrated along Breakers Avenue. A secluded hotel entrance along the south frontage brings guests into the property, while opposite, a dedicated residential lobby activates the north streetscape and provides residents with a personal experience of arriving home.

Along the exterior of the podium, large, landscaped terraces project from the building interior, serving as extensions to the indoors and offering programable areas for breakout spaces, parties, and other events. At these terraces, the enveloping Nest facade rises and falls to create large apertures in areas that open views to the surroundings and bring interior activity outward. In other areas, the Nest serves as a trellis, creating comfortably shaded zones and protecting the interiors from the intense Florida sun.

The form of the building's 24-story tower morphs organically, rising from its square base to its slender, circular top. Across twelve floors of hotel suites and six floors of branded residences, corner windows soften into rounded perimeters, reaching a pure circle at the building's peak. Here a rooftop bar within a circular lazy river provides bathers uninterrupted views of the city, all beneath a crowning metallic ring that reflects the light and energy of the rooftop to viewers below while creating an unmistakable silhouette.

The Nest is both an iconic oceanfront property and an activator of the area's streetlife.

The podium structure transitions in
scale, connecting with the surrounding
urban fabric.

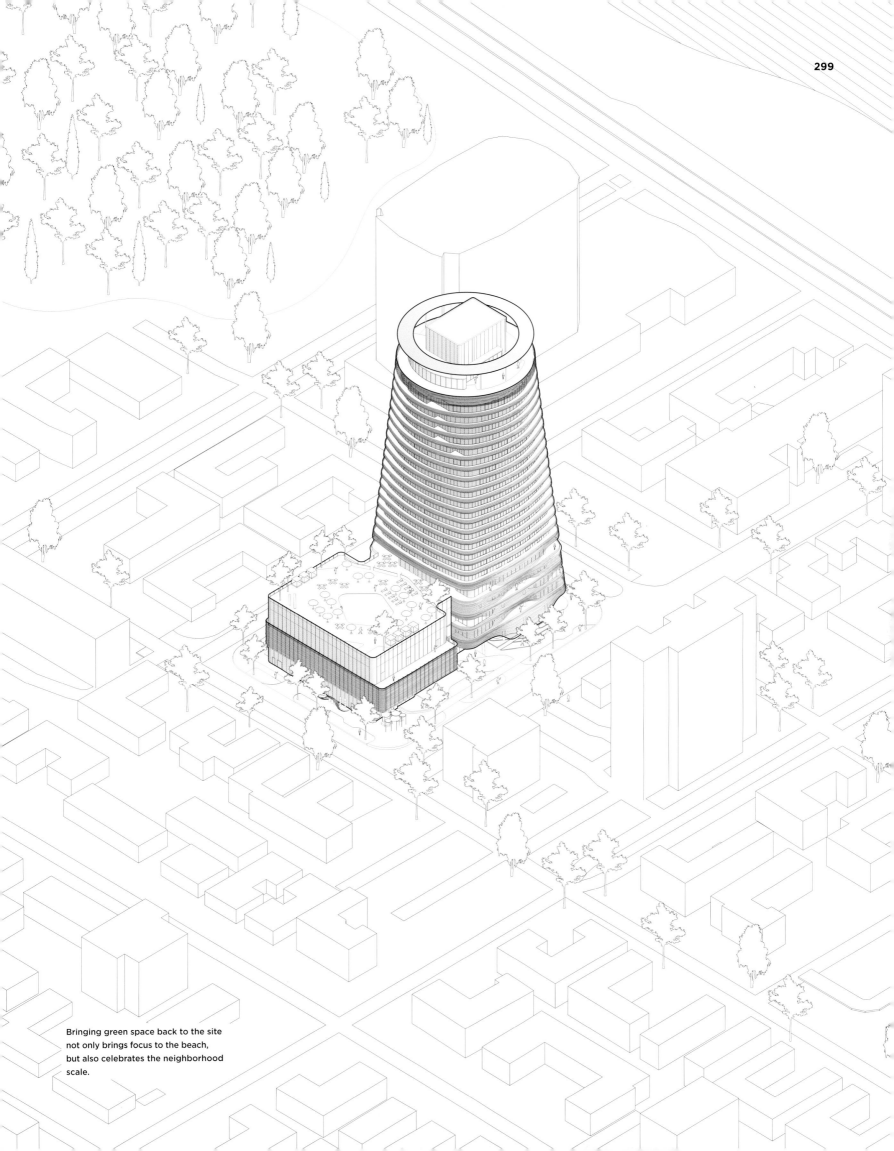

Bringing green space back to the site
not only brings focus to the beach,
but also celebrates the neighborhood
scale.

The building's exterior is composed
of natural-toned aluminum bands that
envelope its balconies and terraces.

LOCATION	740 Eighth Avenue, New York, NY
CLIENT	Extell Development
SIZE	875,372 SF
TEAM	Eran Chen, Michael Unsicker, Katherine Mendez, Pablo Zepeda, Jacob Hedaya, Alex Tahinos, Anirudh Chandar, Michelle Le, Dan Hoch, Julia Fidelis

THE TORCH

In Times Square, arguably New York City's most iconic area, how can a new structure make an impact? The cacophony of these hectic streets may seem to demand something loud that can compete with the flashing lights and advertising pitches of its neighbors, but it offers potential to become a billboard for a much more valuable message: an extension of the public realm in the sky.

Positioned in midtown Manhattan, the design of the Torch capitalizes on its location along Eighth Avenue, between the high-rise, high-density areas of Times Square to the east and the low-rise buildings of Hell's Kitchen to the west.

Inspired by the iconic tops of the city's most famous buildings, the Torch makes a bold statement while adding to the city's skyline. The faceted, highly reflective glass facade provides a unique expression on both the exterior and interior. Enhancing the individuality of the interior experience, every facet of the facade expands the envelope and provides pockets of space for visitors to literally occupy the edge of the building. On the exterior, the play of light across the varying angles of the facade throughout the day creates an ever-changing aesthetic. The facade is interrupted at two key moments expressing the vertical experience on the exterior. The exposed observation deck levels offer oversized stairs, akin to the gathering space of steps at the Met, but 600 feet in the air. The clean lines and transparent glass of the crown reflects the interior program, glowing like a beacon on the skyline.

The Torch aims to extend the public realm into the sky and invites visitors to take a trip through an atmospheric environment, with a play between digital installations and physical materials enhancing the experience. Here, the theme takes its cue from the facade with light being the connecting element. Visitors enter from the ground floor before descending to the cellar beneath a cloud-like ceiling installation complete with a rainfall water feature. Dark natural materials and dramatic floating concrete installations captivate the senses as visitors progress through the cellar, before entering the high-speed elevators to the observation deck at the top of the tower. On the way up, visitors have the option of a one-of-a-kind experience, an amusement park style, giant drop ride that slowly ascends 300 feet in glass tubes before releasing to a free fall.

Arriving at the observation deck, visitors are greeted by 360-degree skyline views, enhanced by a highly digital experience that puts them into the clouds. Visitors continue their experience descending through two more levels of observation decks connected by an exterior amphitheater space.

The Torch envisions a vertical experience like no other. Perched atop a 600-foot-tall hotel, an observation tower extends an additional 500 feet into the sky, combining a three-level, spiraling indoor and outdoor observation deck, a two-level restaurant, and a VIP lounge, all encapsulated in a glass crown.

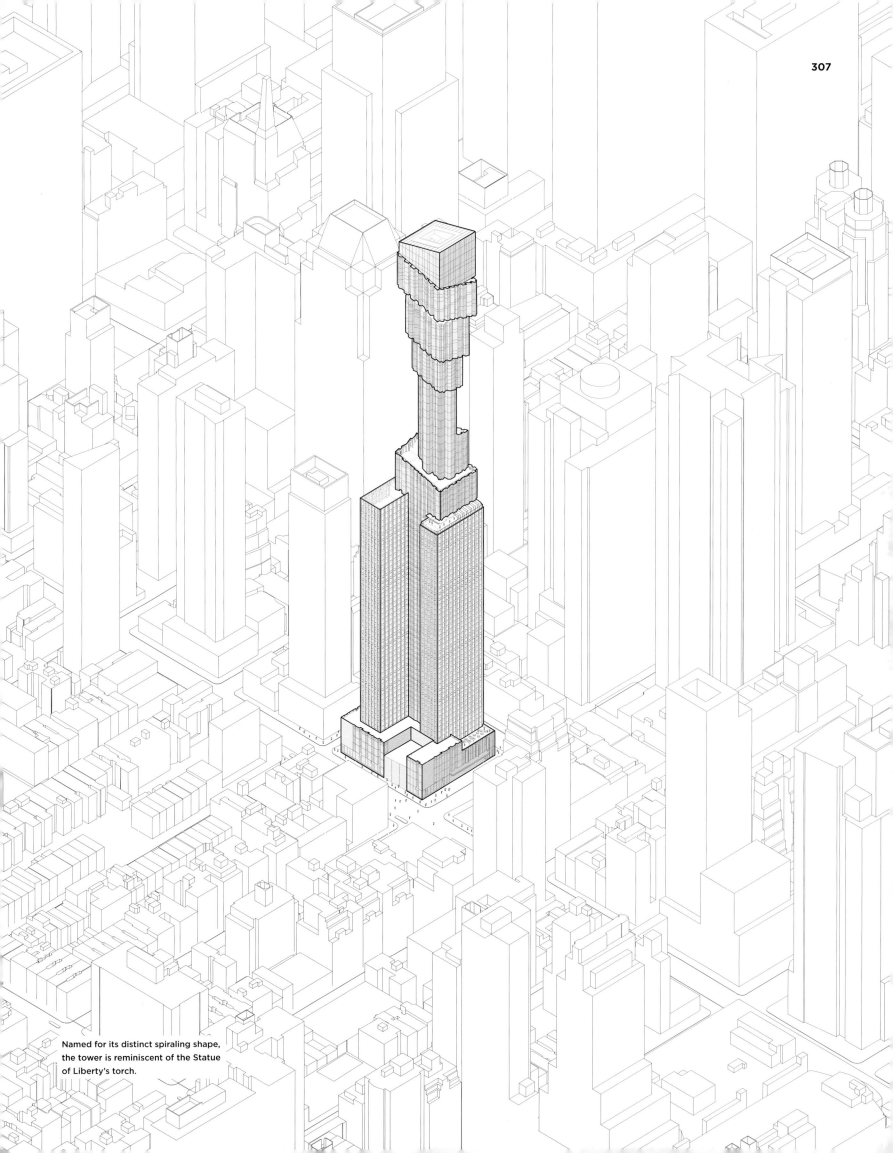

Named for its distinct spiraling shape,
the tower is reminiscent of the Statue
of Liberty's torch.

308

Spiraling slices on the observation deck level expose guests to the outdoors, blurring the boundaries between inside and out 600 feet in the air.

ACKNOWLEDGMENTS

At ODA, we ask ourselves, what makes our cities so great? How can we make them better?

I'd like to tell you a personal story that profoundly shaped my view on the future of urban renewal.

When I was 10 years old, I lived with my mother in a social housing project in the southern city of Israel called Be'er Sheva.
Our residential complex consisted of three six-story row houses, forming a U-shape around a courtyard.
All the apartments had balconies facing inward.
For us as kids, this courtyard was a multigenerational place of experience.

Every day, my friends and I would get back from school and play in the courtyard.
My mom, who worked in a lab at the time, would come from work, make dinner, and call me home from the balcony.
But she didn't call out my name, instead, she would whistle...
Yes, we had our own whistle, like an ancient ringtone.

And here is the amazing part: all my friends and their moms had their own whistles as well.
Each one was unique.
And so, every day between five and six o'clock in the afternoon the courtyard would come alive with a symphony of whistles, and with this enchanting sound we all knew that our playtime was over, and it was time to go home.

This courtyard of whistling moms is my strongest childhood memory.
Those courtyards were the heart of our neighborhood.
And the activities they facilitated were the life of our community.

It is these small moments that cultivate larger life choices, the physical paths that become metaphorical ones. This is what we think good architecture creates; the memories of spaces that we look back on and see as monumental should not be a privilege in the urban environment, but a universal right for all.

I'd like to thank my mother for being my forever source of inspiration, my team for their tireless dedication to our cause, and all the city dwellers of today and tomorrow: families, kids, and whistling moms alike.

CREDITS

FOUNDER

Eran Chen AIA

PRINCIPALS

Dongyoung Kim
Olivera Grk AIA
Michael Unsicker AIA
Ryoko Okada
P. Christian Bailey (2007–2023)

DIRECTORS

Chris Berino
Gene Pyo
Patricia Gortari
Katherine Mendez
Francois Blehaut
Haroon Yousaf

ASSOCIATES

Joanna Regiec
Christopher Sjoberg
Audrey Topp
Alex Tehranian
Jessica Schoen
Jacob Hedaya
Michelle Le

**NEW YORK OFFICE
(2007–2023)**

Ariela Abreu Diaz
Adebowale Adeniyi
Matt Adler
Benjamin Albury
Reut Alegresi
Naeera Ali
Sara Alvarez
Sherisse Alvarez
Eric Anderson
Francesco Asaro
Nofar Ashuri
Mohammad Askarzadeh
Alonso Ayala
Shraddha Balasubramaniam
Ryan Barnette
Mark Bearak
Jean-Baptiste Berteloot
David Bess
Prachi Bhinde
Sharon Blaustein
Aaron Blum
Matt Boker
Lilach Borenstein
Yuval Borochov
Katinka Bosch
Jason Bourgeois
Hadas Brayer
Charles Brill
Julia Bruxel
Zackary Bryson
Frank Bua
Lakshmi Budhu
Mihai Buleu Hoza
Abigail Bullard
Soo Bum
Seung Bum Ma
Flora Burdock
Charles Burke
Kelly Burke
Keith Burns
Michael Cafiero
Fang Cai
Marc Calvet Canal
George Carranza
Ulises Castillo
David Cazares
Amy Cha
Anirudh Chandar
Lynn Charoenchai
Ching-Lun Chen
Ien-Jung Chen

Vladimir Chervoniuk
Ilya Chistiakov
Hyun Jun Cho
Yongchun Choi
Yoonah Choi
Jae Hong Chung
Cedric Cranko
Amaya D'Souza
Filippo Dal Maso
Lisa Del Percio
Maryam Delshad
Charmee Donga
Jamie Edinjiiklian
Caleb Ehly
Jennifer Endozo
Charlotte Ensign
Wayne Erb
Christopher Esper
Matias Estrany y Gendre
Karen Evans
Michael Evola
Roman Falcon
Keren Feilgut
Julia Fidelis
Sunny Fok
Ruth Frommer
Evgenya Fuks
Taylor Fulton
Erin Galvin
Cynthia Gellman
Eric Gellman
Yashar Ghasemkhani
Julia Godsmark
Charles Hajj
Emine Halefoglu
Kevin Hall
Matt Hallstein
Nathan Harelson
Paz Harlev
Jacob Hedaya
Christina Hefferan
Ninoshka Henriques Cukar
Ivan Heredia
Adelle Hernandez
Sofia Herrero
Maria Jose Herrero Gonzalez
Racheli Hershcovich
Dan Hoch
Shin-Yau Huang
Sonia Huang
Aykut Imer
Elizabeth Jackson
Travers Jakimczyk

Tamara Jamil
Philip Jenkin
Min Soo Jeon
Boyuan Jiang
Colin Joyce
Celia Julve Rodriguez
Boram Lee Jung
Dawoon Jung
Yunhwan Jung
Ivan Kam
Gregory Kamback
Saranya Kanagaraj
Kristina Kesler
Arielle Khosla
Jayeon Kim
Joseph Kim
June Kim
Paul Kim
Sejung Kim
Suyoun Kim
Taesoo Kim
Amit Kochen
Steven Kocher
Natalie Komolmis
Tyler Koraleski
Adi Krainer
Chris Krambias
Lindsey Krug
Kyriakos Kyriakou
Brianna Lazzaro
Boram Lee
Brian Lee
Dohyung Lee
Eun Kwang Lee
Joeun Lee
Sunggu Lee
Caroline Lenfant
Kris Levine
Piotr Lewicki
Chris Li
Ching Yen Lin
Tulika Lokapur
Chiekh Loume
Tal Lukman
Seungbum Ma
Ada Macdonald
Erin Marcheski
Ariana Medina
Côme Ménage
Reyha Mete
Adrienne Milner
Melissa Montan
Carolina Moscoso

Josep Mosquea
James Moulder
Kevin Muni
Noah Myers
Paola Naves
Vi Nguyen
Konrad Nieradka
Jamie Niver
Chanho Noh
Kevin O'Connor
Natsumi Oba
Ala Ohadi
Andreas Palfinger
Boliang Pan
Kirat Pandher
Jae Min Park
Max Park
So Jin Park
Christopher Payan
Nitzan Pedut
Belen Pena
Arta Perezic
Tzara Peterson
Dominique Petit-Frere
Emma Pfeiffer
Alexandra Polier
Christopher Pounds
UnJae Pyon
Naama Rabban
Marie-Line Ranschaert
Sneha Ravani
Tanvi Reddy
Caroline Remignon
Katie Rodes
Carolina Rodriguez Gonzalez
Matthew Rosen
Alex Rossetti
Or Rotariu
Hila Sachs
Keith Sagliocca
Kate Samuels
Alexandria Sandhu
Alex Sarria
Gökçe Saygın Batista
Tom Segev
Joohwan Seo
Yaarit Sharoni
Alexandra Sharry
Hayden Shin
Elizabeth Snow
Lilia Sodre Pereira
Oscar Solarte
Diego Soto Madrinan

Rachel Spampinato
Bernhard Stocker
Lois Suh
Akshay Surana
Jowita Szeliga
Alex Tahinos
Diana Tao
Asuncion Tapia
Janet Thai
Heidi Theunissen
Georgina Tiernan
Joana Torres
Khue Truong
Nathan Tunkelrot
Sonia Turk
Nazli Unsal
Juan Urrutia
Sudarshan Venkatraman
Brona Waldron
Stacey Walters
Mingchao Wan
Chia-Min Wang
Chuan Wang
Yutian Wang
Alex Ward
Matthew Wasnewsky
Nai Wong
Woody Wu
Joshua Wujek
Michael Wysochanski
Teng Xing
Yinxing Xu
Seonhee Yoon
Soo Bum You
Shani Zana
Zachary Zeller
Pablo Zepeda
Chencong Zhang
Liwan Zhang
Ruomei Zhang
Shixiao Zhang
Jacqueline Zhao

**BUENOS AIRES OFFICE
(2022–2023)**
Agustin Biggeri
Ignacio Fernandez
Julieta Fernandez
Marcelo Grendene
Nicolas Viterbo

PHOTO CREDITS

12–13: Scott Frances
17–27: Frank Oudeman
29–39: Scott Frances
40–41: Pavel Bendov
45: Scott Frances
46–47: Erieta Attali
48–53: Frank Oudeman
55: Miguel de Guzman
56 (TOP): Dan Balilty
56 (BOTTOM): Miguel de Guzman
58–59: Miguel de Guzman
61: Pavel Bendov
62–63: Miguel de Guzman
64: Pavel Bendov
66–71: Miguel de Guzman
72–75: Frank Oudeman
77–85: Pavel Bendov
87: Miguel de Guzman
88–89: Scott Frances
90 (TOP): Frank Oudeman
90 (BOTTOM) : Miguel de Guzman
92: Miguel de Guzman
93 (TOP): Frank Oudeman
93 (BOTTOM): Miguel de Guzman
94–95: Scott Frances
96–97: Miguel de Guzman
99–110: Aaron Thompson
112–113: Courtesy of Landsea Homes & Sara Fox
115–123: Aaron Thompson
124: Michael Young
125: Aaron Thompson
127–129: Scott Frances
130: Angela Sun
132–141: Scott Frances
143–153: Aaron Thompson
154: Pavel Bendov
159: Miguel de Guzman
160–162: Alon Sicherman
164: Eric Laignel
165: Miguel de Guzman
166 (TOP LEFT, TOP RIGHT, BOTTOM LEFT): Miguel de Guzman
166 (BOTTOM RIGHT): Eric Laignel
167: Miguel de Guzman
168 (TOP): Miguel de Guzman
168 (BOTTOM): Eric Laigne
169: Eric Laignel
170–175: Miguel de Guzman
177–179: Pavel Bendov
180 (TOP): Pavel Bendov
180 (BOTTOM): Alon Sicherman
182–187: Pavel Bendov
189: Albert Vecerka

190–191: Miguel de Guzman
192–194: Petrini Studio
195–203: Albert Vecerka
205–208: James Ewing
210–211: Christian Horan
213–221: Scott Frances
222–223: Pavel Bendov
225: Jason Keen
226: Rebekah Witt
228: Jason Keen
229–231: Rebekah Witt
232–233: VERO
237–245: Forbes Massie Studio
246: The Greypixel
247: V1
248–249: The Greypixel
250–251: Forbes Massie Studio
253–259: Secchi Smith
260–261: Brick Visual
262–263: Secchi Smith
265–273: VERO
275–277: Secchi Smith
278: Israel Teper Arquitectos
280–305: Secchi Smith
306–309: Hayes Davidson
310 (TOP): DN8
310 (BOTTOM): Hayes Davidson
311–313: Hayes Davidson

First published in the United States of America in 2024 by
RIZZOLI INTERNATIONAL PUBLICATIONS, INC.
300 Park Avenue South, New York, NY 10010
www.rizzoliusa.com

Publisher: Charles Miers
Editor (for Rizzoli): Douglas Curran
Production Manager: Colin Hough Trapp
Managing Editor: Lynn Scrabis
Design Manager: Olivia Russin
Proofreader: Sarah Stump

Edited by Julia van den Hout, Original Copy
Project Manager: Kelly Burke, ODA

Designed by Claudia Brandenburg, Language Arts

Cover: Miguel de Guzman, Imagen Subliminal

Printed in Hong Kong
2024 2025 2026 2027 2028 / 10 9 8 7 6 5 4 3 2 1

ISBN-13: 978-0-8478-9953-1
Library of Congress Control Number: 2023940897

Visit us online:
Facebook.com/RizzoliNewYork
Twitter: @Rizzoli_Books
Instagram.com/RizzoliBooks
Pinterest.com/RizzoliBooks
Youtube.com/user/RizzoliNY
Issuu.com/Rizzoli